MIND OVER TERROR

3 WEEKS, 2 CITIES, 1 MISSION

MIND OVER TERROR

3 WEEKS, 2 CITIES, 1 MISSION

DOV BENYAACOV-KURTZMAN RSW
BA, LLB, BSW, PGDIP PSYCHIATRY

Matador
9 Priory Business Park,
Wistow Road, Kibworth Beauchamp,
Leicestershire. LE8 0RX
Tel: 0116 279 2299
Email: books@troubador.co.uk
Web: www.troubador.co.uk/matador
Twitter: @matadorbooks

ISBN 978 1789016 635

British Library Cataloguing in Publication Data.
A catalogue record for this book is available from the British Library.

Printed and bound by CPI Group (UK) Ltd, Croydon, CR0 4YY
Typeset in 12pt Sabon MT by Troubador Publishing Ltd, Leicester, UK

Matador is an imprint of Troubador Publishing Ltd

Dedicated to
my parents, who always stood
by me in everything I have done and
my children, whom I will always stand by.

A special thank you to
Lloyd and Rachael Faber, who provided me
with the first three tiers of Maslow's hierarchy
of needs when I needed them the most.
Jo Watson, who coached me
and taught me how to write.
The acceptance and commitment therapy/training
community and my mentors who taught me how to
accept my inner uncomfortableness, commit to
my values and at the same time take valued
action towards what is important.

I couldn't have materialised this project
without HaShem's personal providence, and
the support, contributions and dedication of:

Miriam (Isolde) Ben Hirsch-Gornemann
Maurice Bennaim
Anthony Hodari
Adam Leighton
Brian McCallum
Anthony Mellor
Barry Parker
Richard Ward
and all our wonderful volunteers.

In a place where one is able to do good and be a worthy person, one should strive to be that person.

[Jewish sage, Pirkei Avot, Mishnah 2:5]

CONTENTS

More than anything else, this book, *Mind Over Terror*, offers an authentic description of the experience from the rare perspective of a person who provides primary assistance, such as Dov. His perspective gives a glimpse of a large variety of personal, individual and community aspects shaped by a terror attack. The description is sober and accurate, making the book unique.

Dr Moshe Farchi, PhD
Originator of the Six Cs Psychological First Aid model
Founder and Head of Stress, Trauma and Resilience Studies in the Department of Social Work, Tel-Hai College, Israel

Dov Benyaacov-Kurtzman is a deep and compassionate human soul (a rabbi and clinical social worker), with immense pragmatism, energy, coherent direction and a sense of justice.

Dov is a dear colleague and friend, who I learned to work with under stressful conditions due to the dark sides of humanity – during the aftermath of terrorism.

His book, *Mind Over Terror*, is a personal account of the work his new organisation has done in the aftermath of terrorist attacks and fires in the UK. *Mind Over Terror* bridges our scientific work with practical help and personal experiences, making it accessible to non-professional and professional readers alike. The book mentions the scientific underpinnings of the interventions we taught therapists, together with many unique examples from Dov and his staff. His style is deep, direct, but also compassionate. His book and his staff's work are to be blessed and remind us about the nice side of humanity.

Professor Yori Gidron, PhD
Chair of Psycho-oncology, University of Lille, France

Mixing his personal story with the social story we all see unfolding on our television screens, this book helps you understand how and why CORTEX-cognitive psychological first aid tries to help people manage the aftermath of terror by moving from chaos to coherence. In the world in which we live, we need mental skills to manage the impact of terror – all of us!
    This book can help.

Steven C. Hayes, PhD
Co-developer of Acceptance and Commitment Therapy
Foundation Professor of Psychology, University of Nevada, US

I believe that this book, *Mind Over Terror*, by Dov Benyaacov-Kurtzman, can be a key resource to any person out there who has a desire to help people's mental wellbeing in the aftermath of trauma and shock, and I stand by the claim that such training can be, and should be, as easy to access as any standard first aid course available in the world today.

Professor Mooli Lahad, PhD
Founding President of the International Stress Prevention
Centre, Kiryat Shmona, Israel
Professor of Psychology at Tel-Hai College, Israel
Previously Visiting Professor of Dramatherapy, University of
Surrey, England

Dov Benyaacov-Kurtzman has written this book from the heart. He has portrayed here his big-hearted view that in these troubled times we can all help, and when we do we grow stronger. His work is enormously important and a shining light to us. His work shows that valued action, small or big, can bring us together and help healing. Together. This is a wonderful read for anyone who has an open heart and wants to discover how to use it.

Louise Hayes, PhD
Author of *The Thriving Adolescent* and *Get Out of Your Mind
and Into Your Life for Teens.*

As terror and trauma unfortunately become more commonplace in our lives, this timely book offers an elixir that will ease global suffering.

Dov Benyaacov-Kurtzman, a brilliant renaissance man with a wealth of training and experience in several disciplines, graces readers with his wisdom on topics ranging from religion, terrorism and the military, to empowerment and personal development.

The cutting-edge six-pronged approach to Cognitive First Aid training offered by his Heads Up Programme quickly and effectively brings survivors of psychological shock from helplessness to effective functioning.

This book is an invaluable resource for anyone who is interested in helping fellow human-beings reclaim their wholeness after experiencing trauma.

Mavis Tsai, PhD, Co-author of *A Guide to Functional Analytic Psychotherapy: Awareness, Courage, Love and Behaviorism;* Research Scientist and Clinical Faculty, University of Washington.

FOREWORD

Let us imagine Bambi, the young deer, grazing peacefully. Suddenly, a tiger jumps at him. Bambi breaks into a run and finds shelter. Is the situation traumatic for Bambi? What does that run mean? Is he escaping, fighting? Our intuitive reply would be that Bambi is on the run, and of course, the situation is traumatic for him.

One day in October 2003, I was walking in the campus of the Tel-Hai College, my academic home, chatting with Dr Atalya Mussak, Head of the Social Work Department. "Congratulations on receiving your PhD, Moshe," she said. "What research seminar would you like to teach?"

"Something to do with children at risk, of course," I replied with confidence. "After all, this is the topic of my doctoral dissertation."

"I'm sorry, that's impossible. I am already giving this seminar. I'd rather you found another topic..."

I thought for a minute about potentially interesting topics, and said, "Well then, perhaps a seminar on trauma could also be interesting." That is how, on a bright summer morning stroll, I boarded one of the most fascinating subjects in the field of intervention.

In 2003, trauma literature dealt mainly with post-trauma, its various symptoms and assistance methods.

I had done some reading on post-traumatic stress disorder (PTSD), but my first interest was the onset of the process rather than its later stages. The literature offered some marginal discussions of acute stress reaction (ASR), describing it as a reaction that starts a process of deterioration. However, the knowledge in this field was scant, and almost never based on evidence. I failed to understand why most of the literature dealt with PTSD and ways to assist those who suffered from this syndrome, rather than dealing with earlier stages, such as that of ASR.

The answer turned out to be simple. At that time, the therapists' milieu did not ascribe any importance to early interventions because most of the treatment doctrines were directed solely at PTSD. At that time – and to some extent even today – a successful treatment of trauma meant reducing post-traumatic symptoms.

I felt that figuring out what happened in the acute stages of what was perceived as trauma would be more interesting and significant than waiting for the chronic stages of PTSD.

In cases of acute stress, initial treatment included calming down the patients, seeing to their basic needs, comforting them, removing them from the event scene and sometimes recommending rest and sleep. In cases of further deterioration, medications were prescribed. Whenever I followed that procedure, I noticed an interesting phenomenon: while the patients were very happy to be helped, and were pleased to rest and take the role of aid recipients, their condition worsened, and they kept developing various other symptoms that required further treatment.

I soon realised that this mode of intervention was somehow wrong. I decided to go back to the beginning and recheck the definitions. To my surprise, discovering the failure turned out to be easy. A quick scan of the *Diagnostic and Statistical Manual of Mental Disorders* (DSM-4) revealed three main factors that define an event as a trauma when they coincide: threat, helplessness and extreme fear (DSM-4, criterion A). Clearly, of those three factors there was nothing to be done with the threat because the event had already happened. Fear and helplessness lingered. Fear never occurs of itself, and never without a reason. In this case, behind fear lies helplessness. This means that all we have to do is reduce helplessness! As simple as that! The opposite of helplessness is effective action in the face of a threat. Once this is achieved, the chain reaction stops! Although this seems so simple, we have been doing just the opposite until now: calming down, isolating, offering water, hugging, speaking softly as if to a small child – in short, we increased the passivity of the involved persons, and made them even more helpless. We worsened their condition with our own hands, instead of improving it.

This set off a speedy process of thought and implementation, until in winter 2011, I presented to the Israel Defense Forces mental health staff my Six Cs model, designed to promptly alleviate acute distress conditions and enable regaining the ability to function effectively. Underlying the model are six principles, all beginning with the letter C: Cognition, Communication, Challenge, Control, Commitment, Continuity. The model was immediately adopted, and two years later became an inseparable part of a soldier's basic training.

Dr Tal Levi Bergman, Head of the Mental Health Division at the Israeli Ministry of Health, joined in the effort, and together we launched a long process at the end of which the Six Cs model was declared in Israel a national model of mental first aid.

In 2016, my secretary asked if she could arrange a meeting for me with Rabbi Dov Benyaacov-Kurtzman. I was happy to meet him again.

That meeting yielded a significant and welcome cooperation with Dov, particularly in 2017 with his Heads Up CIO non-profit organisation. By coincidence (some say coincidences do not exist), our close cooperation came about a year ahead of the 2017 terror attack in Manchester Arena.

More than anything else, this book, *Mind Over Terror*, offers an authentic description of the experience from the rare perspective of a man who provides primary assistance, such as Dov. His perspective gives a glimpse of a large variety of personal, individual and community worlds of content shaped by a terror attack. The description is sober and accurate, making the book a unique one.

Bambi – like all of us – struggles to survive. The only way for him to achieve this goal is by running. The ability to run is his main – perhaps only – coping resource. Bambi uses this resource effectively. He fights!

Is Bambi traumatised? As already mentioned, trauma is made up of a threat and helplessness that together breed fear. Bambi runs, and therefore is not helpless. Although the event was extremely threatening, Bambi fought and won. The event was not a trauma. Bambi continues to function normally.

Early intervention in acute states of stress is meant to simply return a person to normal and effective functioning on the scene of the event. Therefore, whenever we see a person in distress, we should be encouraged to take effective action. Doing this is a Mitzvah, obligated good deed!

Dr Moshe Farchi

Originator of the Six Cs Psychological First Aid model

Founder and Head of Stress, Trauma and Resilience Studies in the Department of Social Work, Tel-Hai College, Israel

THE WHY
AND
THE WHO

I believe that this book can be a key resource to any person out there who has a desire to help people's mental wellbeing in the aftermath of trauma and shock, and I stand by the claim that such training can be as easy to access as any standard first aid course available in the world today.

The book is not designed to be technical or political in any way, but to serve as a narrative of events in the documentation of why and how Heads Up Charitable Incorporated Organisation (CIO) came to be so important in the context of a nurturing society in the form of human beings coming together to support their fellow beings – explicit proof of the power of people helping people, primarily through the application of CORTEX-cognitive psychological first aid (CORTEX-CPFA).

* * *

I was born and raised in Glasgow in Scotland and although I am proud of that fact (especially my accent),

1

I wanted to move abroad as a young adult to work, study and raise a family. Growing up as the only Jewish boy in my school in Glasgow meant that I felt an outsider to my non-Jewish peers and unable to engage fully in my own culture or in theirs. My differences meant that I was bullied for many years. Moving to Israel, especially after having visited there many times on holiday, was such an important draw in my life.

However, in 2016, I returned to the UK in the hope of bringing home one of the most important and unique concepts in health and wellbeing with me.

My vision was to set up a charity that would help people who needed treatment and support in mental health, yet I knew that in the UK people could wait anything from six months to two years to be properly assessed and treated for mental health conditions. In my opinion, the sooner that such people can be treated the better to avoid further or ongoing complications. The charity I wanted to set up would allow anyone who was suffering from mental health issues to access support in a much quicker timeframe. Obviously, this would be quite a substantial project, and so naturally the process I needed to go through was long and heavy going. However, I was fortunate to have friends and contacts who could at least help me with the initial applications to get the charity off the ground. I did at this point think that once I had the status, the funding would come easily. I was wrong. Despite this, I was encouraged both by the support of knowledgeable professionals and the very noticeable gap in services that sadly the National Health Service (NHS) was, and still is, unable to fill. I believed I could contribute to reduce that burden. I still do.

Originally, it had been my plan to set up clinics that could be accessible to patients in the same way that they would access a GP – by calling up to make an appointment that could be fulfilled in a (relatively) short period of time. Patients would be able to self-refer and would not need to wait lengthy periods to follow processes associated with referrals and assessments through the traditional diagnostic routes.

I quickly realised that this project would be a massive undertaking, and that logistically I wouldn't really know who or how to prioritise in such a broad field, and so I drew upon my time and experience abroad to carve out a niche for supporting those who I believed needed mental health support the most urgently. I wanted to work to provide services to those who were affected by, and witnesses to, trauma and shock. For example, those who had been involved in – or in proximity to – events including mass casualties or severe physical trauma, such as a terrorist attack, a fire or a train crash. I wanted the charity to focus on treatment in emergency psychological shock response, but in the spring of 2017, it became clear that the charity would need to become even more focused than that – in the immediate aftermath of terrorist attacks.

Shortly after getting the go ahead from the Charity Commission to set up my project, I spent the first three or four months of 2017 thinking about how exactly I was going to implement my work. In the meantime, though, having not been back in the country long and having somewhat of a 'new' life to lead, I wanted and needed to make a living for myself. As a result, I started up my own business delivering commercial training to businesses and organisations that would benefit from knowledge and application of emergency protocols in CORTEX-CPFA.

Four years previously, in 2012, I retired early from my career. I was rarely home, and this had put added strain on my marriage, which I would only see in hindsight. The intensity of my job and the impact it had on my home life all built up to form quite a large stress in my life. I believed that we had a wonderful marriage and so the shock of the 'sudden' breakdown had a significant effect on me and meant that I suffered more than a degree of trauma. I initially struggled to cope, but I would ultimately use all my new learning and experience to give me the necessary foundations for helping myself and the mental health and wellbeing of others – those whose experience of trauma would be far more severe.

Two weeks prior to my leaving date, my boss had told me I'd need to use up my holiday allocation. Part of the deal in the organisation I worked for was that they paid for a holiday for you, wherever you wanted to go in the country. As a result, I accepted the gift of a few days away at a spa hotel up in the mountains overlooking the sea. A spa hotel wouldn't usually have been my first choice of holiday, but I was willing to accept the option as I thought it may do some good for my difficult relationship with my wife, as unfortunately, we were very much in the aftermath of an acute marital problem. With hindsight, her behaviour could have been caused by the fact that I was never at home with my family, owing to the travelling

I needed to do with my job. Seeing as I was retiring early from my dream job in a drastic move, this problem of my absence would be eradicated, but there was a lot of damage already done within the marriage.

Arriving at the hotel, you could see many guests wandering around in robes and slippers, and I arrived smoking a cigarette. It wasn't a great start. To add to this, the forecast predicted rain for the four days we would be away. Subsequently, I almost felt obliged to sign up to taster sessions and workshops that the hotel was running to promote health and wellbeing, as I believed that these would at least pass the time. Hopefully, they would also prove to be a good bonding opportunity with my wife. Tai chi, meditation, aromatherapy... none of these had ever interested me before, but I would give them a go. I ended up going to pretty much all the workshops that were on offer, as it transpired that my wife and I couldn't even build a conversation if left to our own devices.

It was a very stressful time in my life. I know it sounds a little radical, but honestly, the session I had in the meditation workshop would go on to change my life. There was something about lying on the floor on my back just being quiet that put me in a much simpler place – like being at the end of a Physical Education lesson at primary school. Lying there in that session, hearing the rain fall outside on the roof, it occurred to me that this was the first time in a long time that I'd stopped and taken some moments where I'd just done nothing but enjoy the stillness. It felt alien, but it felt good.

Upon leaving the meditation session, I wanted to find out more. As soon as I got back home a few days later, I began to research. I found Wingate, a college that taught a four-year course in naturopathy (natural medicine). I signed up straight away. I could have signed up to four years of attending sessions like the one I'd loved at the hotel, but I am the sort of person who loves to learn how to do things myself, rather than have them done *to* me, and this quest for further learning in the field of therapy and psychological wellbeing went on to permeate who I would become and the charity I would set up.

A year later, in 2013, I met a wonderful teacher whilst visiting a prestigious college in Israel: Dr Moshe Farchi. The doctor hailed from the most northerly town in Israel, and amongst other accolades was Head of the Social Work Department at a local college in the middle of a high-profile war-torn area of the world. Dr Farchi is somewhat of a pioneer in dealing with those affected by, and witnesses of, stress and trauma, mainly because the local people were facing either the threat or the aftermath of war and terrorism daily.

That summer in 2013, I had travelled up to the college open day, where I had seen an advert for an introduction course Dr Farchi would be running on psychological first aid. For some reason that I still can't fathom, the only attendee at Dr Farchi's event was *me*. It was a massive shame for the doctor and for the college, because the lack of interest meant that the course didn't go on to run, but it was still a great opportunity for me, as I had the pleasure of having his company to myself for that two-hour period. I learned a significant amount that afternoon and formed a good friendship with a great man. I knew from this moment that this meeting would go on to spark significant ideas for me in my own future.

At the time of meeting Dr Farchi, I had already switched from studying naturopathy to studying for a postgraduate diploma (PgDip) in psychiatry, and was living in a city called Zfat, which is known to be the highest city in Israel. Remotely placed 900m up in the fresh air of the mountains, I had holed myself away in a 200-year-old natural stone house to work hard on my studies. My decision to settle in such a place arose from the fact that I knew my studies were going to be tough and would take a lot of my attention and focus. How did I know this? Because usually, to get on such a high-level course, you need to be a doctor of some sort, or to at least have practised at that level. I was far from being a doctor and cannot claim that I even intended at any point to become one. What I did have was life experience. This mature student status meant that I was less of a risk to the university in terms of likelihood that I would drop out or simply not take my studies seriously. I told the admissions team that I would promise to be one of the most dedicated students they could possibly accept that year. The team saw passion and persistence in me, and, combining some glowing references with a history of being a good student on other courses elsewhere, they accepted me.

I completed my first year on my PgDip Psychiatry with a merit. It was a neuroscience-based induction and facing this level of challenge within my studies would go on to help me later in life for future studies. I finished my second year and earned my PgDip Psychiatry with a distinction and so had kept my promise to the admissions team that I would be one of the most dedicated students they had. Combining this with intensive training to become a marriage guidance counsellor, a cognitive behavioural therapist and a clinical social worker, I was beginning to learn about myself and deal with a lot of stress and trauma that had gone on in my own life.

I couldn't do all of this on my own, however. I had several mentors, having posted on a professional networking site that I wanted to learn from professionals in the field of mental health. Dr Yochi Bennun was a clinical psychologist at Meir Hospital and Head of Israel's Psychological Association. Prior to passing away in 2015, she served as so much more than a mentor to me and became more of a grandmother figure in the process of her support for what I was doing. Dr Miriam (Isolde) Ben Hirsch-Gornemann was my second mentor, and she was a leading scientist in etiology of psychiatric disorders.

Dr Yehuda Baruch also offered to mentor me. He was the Director of Abarbanel Hospital in Bat Yam. He said he'd give me ten minutes of his time in January (this was in November). I accepted his invitation and met with him two months later. During the meeting, like some kind of genie, the good doctor simply asked, "What do you want to learn from me?" I honestly didn't know. I thought about the question and told him that I wanted to know what a psychiatrist really did, and that I wanted to shadow him for a short while. He said no. He then told me that if I was serious about learning what such practices were all about, I would have to attend his hospital for one day a week – every week for a year. I told him I'd give him three years.

And so, I volunteered, one day a week for three years, at

Dr Baruch's psychiatric hospital. It gave me a real practical insight into my studies, and even served as a fantastic placement to fulfil the practical requirements of an additional degree in clinical social work that I had started in 2014. I couldn't get enough of learning, understanding and following the processes of healing. By that time, I was volunteering for three days each week at the hospital.

Whilst at the hospital, I worked with patients who had acute psychosis and simultaneously suffered from substance use disorder (dual diagnosis). I got to see what happened when such patients were involved in legal proceedings, and I saw some truly difficult and always emotional cases. It was very intense and compared to some of the placements my fellow students were on, I was involved in some hard case management and counselling. I learned a lot about the patients I worked with, and I learned not to judge, which was a massive lesson for me to undertake. I researched acceptance and commitment therapy (ACT) with those suffering from dual diagnosis. I did a lot of work on myself and came to really know my stuff, as they say. I loved every minute. It was a privilege.

Traditional approaches to dealing with acute stress reaction (ASR) are very emotion or 'comfort' based and lie within the guidelines of the World Health Organization. We talk with people and ask if they're okay. We offer them a hug, a blanket or a drink to soothe them. We very much operate on the lower levels of Maslow's hierarchy of needs. However, Dr Farchi had taught me that emotional treatment of somebody affected by ASR leads to the person becoming even more emotional about the situation, which in fact doesn't help them. For example, when someone is suffering in such a way in the aftermath or fallout of a critical event, we feel the intuitive desire or need to put our arms around them and engage in reassuring dialogue. Whilst this provides much-needed comfort, psychologically it doesn't help. It sounds cold, but what these people need is to return to function, and so anybody attempting to truly help them needs to trigger the area of the brain known as the pre-frontal cortex. This reduces the emotional effect and therefore allows the person to come back to a functional state, so that they can act and react in a way that is more positive, useful and beneficial to their physical safety and mental wellbeing. It's a wholly cognitive-neurological rather than emotional approach. It's a wonderful breakthrough – if not entirely empathetic in a traditional sense.

In Israel, this triggering of the pre-frontal cortex is taught to every combat soldier and soon will be taught to every professional whose job it is to face or deal with trauma, such as fire-fighters, emergency medical technicians and other first responders. If these people appear to be 'out of commission' because of psychological shock when it strikes, then they would traditionally need to be evacuated from their position at that time. This loss of manpower then has a knock-on effect on the people who require their services in such an event. Here in the UK, training professionals accordingly in CORTEX-CPFA can help them return effective functioning to their colleagues and keep them in active service.

I do not believe that such training should be offered purely to these sorts of professionals, however. Anyone can benefit from the techniques, and just as anyone can learn traditional first aid, anyone can learn CORTEX-CPFA – no professional qualification or background in therapy is required. With the right training, in just two minutes you can bring a person 'back' from the effects of psychological shock, allowing them to cope and, if necessary, to continue with their good work in helping and supporting others. It's no different to CPR in that sense; you're keeping them functioning. So, from January 2017, whilst waiting to see what would or wouldn't happen in the charity's development, I set up a commercial training entity to begin up-skilling people in this field of CORTEX-CPFA. It would at least allow me to be the first to introduce this concept to the UK, if not on the operational charitable basis that I ultimately wanted.

With the business going well, in the early hours of Tuesday 23 May 2017, I was sitting in my living room in my house in Manchester, when a chance turn-on of the television meant that I was faced with the flood of news reports documenting the previous evening's terrorist attack at the Manchester Arena, a venue just a mile or two from where I was sitting. I looked at my phone to see that I had so many messages coming through from across my network. It was well known that I'd been promoting my ideas for training in CORTEX-CPFA on social media, and so I was now receiving messages from people asking me what I was going to do to support the survivors of the attack at the Manchester Arena. I must admit, I wasn't ready!

Even in this day and age, are we *ever* ready for an attack of terrorism?

So, later that day, on the advice of a good friend of mine, Anthony Mellor, who had wanted to support the charity, we travelled the short distance from my home to the vigil in Albert Square in Manchester city centre, where news crews flooded the area to talk with members of the public about the previous evening's confirmed terror attack at the Manchester Arena. I was in a daze, taking in the scenes and the atmosphere in the wake of the attack in this great city where I'd come to feel so safe. I was snapped back into reality, however, when Anthony shoved me in front of a camera crew from a local news station. They interviewed me as a local resident and rabbi, and I began to spread the word to the press and the camera crews that I was going to open a 'pop-up' support centre for survivors, witnesses and those affected by the attack, and that I was going to train local volunteers to aid in their support.

I had no idea how I was going to do this, but I'd put it out in a very public forum now; it would have to go ahead, and the charity would be put to work immediately.

Putting out the word - Albert Square

News interview with BBC

United together in the aftermath of terror

DOV ON... THERAPY

As someone who believes that words have great power, I don't like the word 'therapy'. In modern society, I think the word has connotations of something being wrong with the person who seeks or needs it, and I don't like that it is medicalised and focused on pathology, whereby something can be physically fixed. It's not about that for me, and instead a therapeutic approach should be about the individual, and their journey towards having a better quality of life in their own wellbeing.

Whether I like it or not, however, there's no getting away from its significance.

Although I often underplay my status as a registered practising clinician in the field of therapy, I am someone who, through my own interests and comprehensive high-level studies, is immersed within its world of benefits. In my life I've been able to study, observe and even experience for myself a whole range of different therapies, from the traditional to the alternative, and from the progressive to the somewhat now outdated. Whilst I love the practice, for me, therapy will always be about who is sitting in front of you – the client. Whilst there may be certain therapies that are more appropriate for certain situations, experiences and states, I believe that the wants and needs of the individual are key in selecting and applying the right form of therapy to help them.

In applying any kind of therapy to help somebody, I believe you must do what is right for *them*. You need to help them get what they want, and not what you or a third party thinks that they need. You need to look at the direction they are heading in and work from that point, rather than apply any kind of cover-all product to the course. Everybody has a direction that is useful and holds value for them, but how they journey, and in what timeframe, will be different for everyone.

I think that therapy comes in many forms, and that we all can experience it daily. It doesn't have to be something formal, labelled, or professionally administered and monitored. Everyone can learn simple processes, and everyone has the choice to immerse themselves into whatever context helps them work towards what is important to them. Today, we hear of 'retail therapy', whereby people go shopping to make themselves feel better, perhaps by making a purchase or two. Using therapy in this way can be a quick fix and yet another way of avoidance of the real issues, however, and in my opinion, these rarely work in the long term.

Acceptance and commitment therapy (ACT) is a more experiential approach to dealing with core issues, as differentiated from medication or institutionalisation. On a side note, I don't believe that time spent in mental health institutions does much to treat a person; rather it treats symptoms and keeps its patients safe from harming others and indeed themselves. ACT provides perspectives that can help us to grow, which has always been a key part of my own personal philosophy. Everybody has something they can offer, and in turn, everyone has something that they need.

MY MISSION

E arlier in the day, prior to attending the vigil at Albert
Square, I'd already begun to pave the way for the
part I felt I could play in supporting those affected
by the Manchester Arena terrorist attack the previous
evening. I had been spending the afternoon updating my
social media accounts to announce to people that I really
needed to get things up and running with regards to a
pop-up support centre. Social media would go on to be
the most powerful tool possible in driving forward the
aims and outcomes of the charity. At this point, however,
all posts came from my own personal page. I had not
even got as far as building so much as a Facebook page
for the charity.

With the enormity of what had happened the previous
evening, it was clear that I needed to act quickly, and that
the charity was needed right here, right now. However,
despite the charitable status, I had no money, no contacts,
and no real starting point for what I needed and wanted
to do. I began to contact people that I had met in
Manchester during the months since I had settled there.
I targeted people who I believed would be able to at least
put me in contact with strong networks that would be
able to help me get things off the ground at such a high-

profile and critical time. Surely there would be people out there who would want to help.

At 2.56pm, my good friend Jonny Wineberg contacted me through my Facebook page to put me in touch with a contact of his, Maqsood Ahmad OBE, who happened to be a strategic clinical network manager for the NHS. I had no idea what this job title meant but it was one that led me to believe that this individual could be a person of influence and key support. This contact was a clinical lead for the Clinical Commissioning Group (CCG) in Manchester. I was grateful for him taking the time to speak with me, and I was thankful for his immediate enthusiasm and support. In that window of opportunity, I told him that I wanted to open a 'pop-up' psychological support centre in Manchester city centre, and I wanted to see if the NHS could, or would, help me in some way. I briefed him on my background and knowledge of protocols working within post-terrorist attacks. He said he would see what he could do.

After getting off the phone to Maqsood, I continued to make more phone calls. I called a social worker I knew at a local care organisation, and then called the Chair of a board of governors at a very large secondary school I was familiar with. I was aware that those people may not be able to help me directly, but indirectly they might be able to connect me to people in their networks and circles of influence within key authorities.

When talking to people that day, a question that I was almost always asked within the first 60 seconds of the conversation was, "Are you looking for money?" Well, in some ways I was, because all ventures need financial resource, but this was nowhere near my priority at the time, when a more pressing issue was the need to gather a network. I also wasn't asking for money because I understood that people perhaps didn't have any, or that they were unhappy about giving it to somebody who they had never met or known before, but the question was always surprising because, as I say, I wasn't even asking for any. Maybe I should have just been blunt with each person and indeed asked for money on the off-chance they would want and be able to oblige, but I became more and more adamant that other things were much more of a priority and use to the charity, such as manpower, facilities and exposure. I guess it didn't matter in the end, because nobody came back to me to offer anything.

With conversations ringing through my head, I began to think more in depth about the concept of funding for the mammoth task that was ahead of me. People had been right to ask, it seemed. So, I picked up the phone once more and dialled the number of Barry Parker, a local businessman I had met not long after coming to Manchester. That first meeting with Barry was after he had approached me through a mutual connection in the form of his son, Ryan, when he had wanted to manage a new rehabilitation centre for people with addictions. He had heard about my background and wanted me to be the lead on his project, based out of a private clinic in Manchester. We had been well underway in meetings, envisaging how it may all work, and he had shared his vision with me. Sadly, nothing ever came of it, but we had stayed in touch, and at this point I knew that Barry had two things that I needed: an interest in mental wellbeing, and money. I had nothing to lose, so I called him.

Straight down the line, I told Barry I needed him to find me a property from where to base the pop-up support centre. Then, I told him that I would need him to underwrite any financial costs that would transpire as the project developed. I had nothing to lose. I had raised my ideas with Barry previously, so with a knowledge of what I wanted to do, he told me he would help.

In terms of what kinds of cost Barry would need to cover, I really didn't know, but I anticipated that it would run into the thousands. I didn't need funds right away, but I needed someone to back me. I admit it was all very unorganised, but Barry told me not to worry. He said he would see what he could do about the property, and something about his tone made me feel confident that this would work out.

It was around this point in the day when my friend Anthony called me to tell me about the vigil in Albert Square, an event that would mark 24 hours since the atrocities of the previous night. Anthony was, and still is, a counsellor for addictions. We had become friends after he had seen an interview that I had done with Professor Steven Hayes, who is a pioneer in the field of acceptance and commitment therapy (ACT). I had broadcast the interview on social media two months earlier, and it was then that Anthony had contacted me via similar channels to see if we might do some work together.

Upon returning home from the vigil, I felt tired but hopeful, having spent the day being as productive as I possibly could be to achieve an aim that I believed would be massively beneficial to our community. I felt that I had received some knockbacks for sure, but that I had also made some decent in-roads.

The next day was Wednesday, and it was 1.19pm. Simon Rosenthal, an employee of Barry's, contacted me to fill me in on the progress of my conversation with his employer the evening before. Barry had delegated this project to Simon, and I liked his choice of personnel. Simon told me that there was a possibility that our pop-up centre could operate out of the town hall in Manchester city centre. To build some momentum for everything that was happening, I made this exciting venue announcement on Facebook. It was premature, but I was keen. Unfortunately, the town hall plan didn't materialise, but I stayed positive that something good would happen and that a venue would show up.

In the meantime, I placed an appeal on social media to connect with mental health professionals who may want to donate time and invest energy for the good of Manchester. Ideally, I wanted and needed such people to be familiar with ACT but I knew that this may be casting out too small a net, so it wasn't billed as essential. Communications with Simon hinted that a venue was looking more and more likely, and in terms of having an operational overview of the project, things were really starting to come together after a good friend of mine, Maurice, arrived from abroad to help me.

Later that Wednesday, I went back into the city centre. The night before, some of the interviewers had requested for me to come back to report on a follow-up of my plans. Members of the press were flying about in the aftermath of the events in their droves, and my involvement with them really did have a snowball effect. It was hectic, but the growing exposure was what the charity needed. I think the fact that I was a rabbi maybe helped with the coverage I was getting – a man of religion operating in a contentious scenario born out of belief and extremism. The press were, as a result, keen to ask me if the project was only aimed at the Jewish contingent of the Manchester community. The answer to that was a definitive 'No'. The project was not faith-based in any way. I would never have introduced myself as a rabbi, but Anthony really believed that a faith link would help gather some momentum and add empathy and weight to what we wanted to achieve.

As well as directly propelling me into key pathways, Anthony was also a huge benefit to me as he had some great contacts. One of those contacts was an ACT psychologist called Mark Webster. Mark was well known for utilising ACT within peer recovery for addictions. Mark would go on to be of great help to me as I worked towards getting the charity working for the good of Manchester.

Thinking back to the night of the vigil, I had been heartened by the amount of people I had met and connected with in the wake of one of the worst events to ever happen to the beautiful city of Manchester. I met people from all faiths and communities and listened intently to their stories and views as they were interviewed. So many people wanted to help. It's strange yet comforting how such beautiful things can come of such tragic circumstances. I took photos of my new-found community and shared them on Facebook, along with tags of solidarity and support.

That evening would pretty much mark the start of a month of no sleep. This was only partly due to the natural stresses that facilitating such an intensive project would present, but also because a key advice line for me came in the shape of my close uncle, Norman Evans, who was in a whole other time zone for communication at his home in Toronto. My home would go on to become HQ for the charity and our impending work, and we would work hard to welcome in and speak to people from near and far who could help us.

It was of great importance to me to try to get Dr Farchi to come and join us, whereby he would serve in the role of a trainer to those who we sought to recruit as mental health volunteers helping those in need in the aftermath of the terrorist atrocities. Dr Farchi was unavailable at the time but promised to join our efforts later. What he was able to suggest, however, was his colleague, who was a professor willing and able to join us in the first instance to serve as our trainer. And so, it came to pass that Professor Yori Gidron would be coming over from Belgium within the next few days. His field of vast clinical and academic expertise lay in researching the aftermath of traumatic events, cognitive psychological therapies and post-traumatic stress disorder. His knowledge would be invaluable, and I was delighted that he had so readily agreed to join the team.

On the Thursday, our position was that we were much closer to having a place in which to base our charity, we had volunteers wanting to be trained, and trainers ready to train them! The only issues were the logistics behind getting experienced colleagues across from Israel to help with our operations. I took a big chance and got on the phone to the only two airlines I knew that flew from the international airport in Israel direct to the North West of England – easyJet and Monarch. I wanted to know if they would donate tickets to the cause. This approach is not something that usually sits well with me, but I wondered if this would count as an exceptional cause. I couldn't even get through to Monarch as the number I had been given kept ringing out. I got through to easyJet, but their operatives kept redirecting me everywhere across the continent. Eventually, I got through to a local department that it seemed would be able to help. I explained, and they listened. I told them that I would also be trying to contact Monarch if it wasn't something easyJet could do. It turns out, it was. At 11.29am, I reserved the tickets under the code of MA17 (Manchester Arena 2017) and was sure to praise easyJet for their wonderful act.

At 12.41pm, I spoke to the security company in London, SQR Security, that I'd worked with initially as part of my commercial training work. I told them I needed a vehicle to use as a mobile unit for our operations, and for the second time that day, I got a 'Yes'.

At 9.17pm, Simon called to inform me that we were pretty much set with a venue, and that this would be in the guise of a shop front anonymously donated by a generous donor (whom I will refer to as A. H.) at number 53 Tib Street in Manchester's popular Northern Quarter. I was in Simon's hands and I trusted him to get this wrapped up for us. Even though I'd never seen the place, I had faith. I wanted to start things up and get into the venue straight away to use it for training by Sunday that week. I had anticipated and planned for four or five volunteers to come along for training, even though ideally, I wanted more. As it would turn out, we would carry out our training at a different venue, a place called Phoenix Mill on Percy Street, which a local organisation had donated to our cause. This change of venue was needed because the amount of people confirming via Facebook that they wanted to volunteer was, by this stage, over 70. Amazing! Tib Street was a great venue, but it was, at this point, completely empty and devoid of furnishings. To cater for over 70 people in a professional manner, we would need a purpose-built training facility, and the property on Percy Street was the perfect place.

Friday morning started early – at 1.44am, to be precise. I had just placed the finishing pieces of information on our brand-new website – www.MA17.org.uk. We now had presence, and this would be essential in recruiting support for our charity as a whole, and for our pop-up support centre in particular.

On the Saturday, work on the project continued in my absence, as Jewish teaching does not allow me to partake in work of any kind unless it is an immediate life-saving necessity. In some ways this could have been argued, given the context of what I was working on, but being Jewish is a huge part of my identity, and so I respected the Sabbath. The power of networking had meant that a wonderful team of people around me continued to put things into place for the next day's volunteer training event.

When Sunday came, I set up my phone to transmit a Facebook Live stream from the training event with the first 20 or 30 or so of our 80 volunteers. Another cohort would go through training later in the day, and a third cohort would come through on a session the following day. This was never the initial plan, as I only expected four or five volunteers, but such was the demand for places from people who wanted to help, we needed to put on three training sessions instead of one to meet demand.

It was 9.12am, and though it was only early in the day, it hit me that I was running mainly on adrenaline and the support of such a great team. My friend Maurice had been particularly helpful, as he had organised the training schedule and even went to meet our trainer, Yori, at the airport by himself. In other operations, Sharon Balkin and other friends of mine from past as well as present had offered up their services to welcome and register volunteers on the day, and did this with proper software, too, rather than just a piece of paper that I probably would have used. It was wonderful to draw on strengths, and to remind myself that I had good friends around me.

I love taking active hands-on involvement in projects, but I am the kind of leader who just needs to know that things are being done. I don't like to micromanage people, and instead I empower them and show my trust in them to achieve common goals and to take ownership of their part of the project. I felt confident that this was happening for our training sessions with our volunteers.

The 80 or so volunteers who had come along to the training sessions represented a wonderful diverse community of professionals. Different faiths were represented, as well as different professional medical and therapeutic backgrounds. I think only around 10% were Jewish, which I guess was important in reminding the rest of the community that this was not a Jewish faith-based intervention. The make-up of the room was mainly female, and I would say the age range was roughly between 35 and 60. Almost all met the criteria I had initially set of having amassed at least 100 hours of clinical supervision, and/or holding a minimum Level 4 for counselling or similar. I realised that this is quite precise, which is one of the reasons why I'd initially thought only four or five people would be joining us in fitting this criteria.

Although the stipulation for recruitment had been that the volunteers should come from a professional therapeutic background, there were a few nurses and faith leaders who had also expressed interest, and we were keen to have them involved and thankful of their time, passion and commitment. I often say that anybody can train to learn and administer cognitive psychological first aid. So, why in this case did I only target practising professionals? I guess the answer to that is because I was aware that this was the start of something new, critical and potentially high-profile. I wanted the project and the charity to gain a reputation of credibility, so it was important to me that the first 'run', if you will, was made up of a cohort of professionals in the field.

At the start of each training session, I introduced myself to the group. I told them about me and what I wanted to achieve. I reiterated information that had gone out on the Facebook appeal for volunteers. I told them that I could not put a number on the total hours I would need from them to volunteer, but that the free training was based on their commitment to use and apply their learning after the session in helping at the pop-up centre and/or in our mobile unit. For me, this personal commitment was always going to be just as important as clinical qualification.

The concept of credibility would also be key from the delivery side of operations, and our team was soon to be bolstered by the arrival of Dr Sandi Mann, who is a high-profile media psychologist. Her daughter had been involved in the arena bombing, and so our mission was of great personal significance to her. Sandi was instrumental in liaising with the media ensuring that news of our good work was travelling beyond the walls of our training venue.

A case of attendee-turned-team-member was Dr Susan Louise Iacovou. Such was her passion to volunteer and desire to help the charity and what we were doing, I asked her to go on to become our clinical lead. Susan was a great asset and a friend. It is not lost on me how fortunate I was to operate in such a strong network of those who hold empathy and kindness as well as professional abilities.

Due to the amount of people who had signed up to volunteer, we had planned in a second training day of two cohorts and this took place on the Monday. At 7.57am that day, one hour and three minutes before the training even started, I announced on social media that *two* hours and three minutes later, we would be opening the doors of the pop-up support centre, utilising the services of the volunteers who had gone through their training the previous day. All would be welcome, and our doors would stay open until 6pm that evening. The centre would serve as a safe place for families to come and talk through and deal with their experiences in the aftermath of the attack at the Manchester Arena. The centre would be based at Tib Street as initially planned.

The only problem was that the shop front on Tib Street was still entirely empty. No chairs, no tables, and it was a Bank Holiday Monday.

This was going to be tough.

Training with Professor Yuri Gidron

Participants arriving for training

Volunteers in empty clinic

"An overwhelming response from committed action folk. Amazing people to work with. They are 'don't wait – do it' people. The folks at Mutual Aid are just amazing. Big thanks to Anthony Mellor and Mark Webster. So many people to thank that are working around the clock to make this a successful project for the people affected by the horrendous terror event less than a week ago. To see so many people come together and offer their time and resources is THE ANSWER to terrorism – *No Surrenda Ta Terra!* Building relationships is THE answer. Building and respecting LIFE and not death and distruction. I am truly full of gratitude and appreciation and immensely humbled to lead such a great international team that are self-sufficient, enthusiastic and very very brave. Well done all. xx

Facebook post

DOV ON... RELIGION

I am Jewish. I am practising. I am Orthodox. I am a rabbi. I am active within the Jewish community.

I was educated as a Jewish person from birth and have grown up within its culture both in the UK and in Israel, which is predominantly a country of Jewish people. Being Jewish is synonymous with my identity, and although I see being Jewish as a way of life rather than a religion, I believe that religion, faith or whatever you choose to call it does indeed do much to shape an individual as well as communities. However, I prefer to see my way of life in the context of a relationship expressed through physical obligations and servitude. Life is precious and important.

I had become a rabbi not through vocation or calling, but because I wanted to have a deeper understanding of the Jewish way of life. It also turned out to be a stop on a pathway that was strengthening my bond with my eldest son, Boaz, seeing as he was essentially one of my teachers! Similarly, I would never have thought to even mention my status when I was going about spreading awareness of the Heads Up CIO charity, until I saw how it could add status to a project that promotes the unification of a community and the support of individuals within it. Through faith (*emuna*), I feel a connection to something spiritual that's very deep, and I view G-d to be the source; the higher and only power. Nothing exists outwith G-d. There is an intimate loving relationship, even if it is complex to explain.

In society today, we often automatically mix the concept of religion into the pot when we talk about terrorism. People are quick to blame Islam, and this is not helped when the very people at the heart of the attacks, such as those in the spring of 2017, use that religion as justification for their acts. Terrorism has long been a part of society, but this has more often been linked to politics or movements. Today, terrorism is associated much more closely with religion, and there are in fact very few terrorist groups left that are non-religious-based in their claims. It seems that the two terms of terrorism and religion are, in some cases, now synonymous.

Do I believe that terrorists are religious? I believe that they think they are, but not religious as within any religion that you or I would recognise. These people have been brought up or perhaps indoctrinated into a religion of hate, but hate has no teaching, church or manuscript. Hate has no deity or symbolism of history or tradition. Hate has no gathering together in the hope of nurturing peace and community. So, no, terrorism is not about religion, and we need to separate those terms.

All the work that I have done for Heads Up CIO was not born from a religion, a response to a religion, or based in the principles of a religion, but if it helps bring people together in peace and to help them support each other, then this can only be a good thing.

BUCKINGHAM BUNNIES

L ater that day, Monday 29 May, 8.05am.

I had taken to social media once again and made an announcement that the training for our cause at Heads Up CIO had gone incredibly well and looked set to keep momentum into the day ahead. Along with the announcement, I invited people to get involved with us in any way they could, or to ask questions about what we were doing. I wanted to build a following. I gave all the details once more about the pop-up support centre on Tib Street and encouraged all of our followers to spread the word.

At 10.32am, one of our volunteers, Susan Brock, became the first of our team to post *to* our new Facebook page, as opposed to all communications coming *from* me as the admin on the account. On her post, Susan stated that our mission down at the venue on Tib Street had recruited two community champions for the cause: a community support officer called Al, and a traffic warden named Nathan. The two gentlemen in question had been delighted with what they had seen down at our centre and were keen to spread the word in their community about what our volunteers could do to support others who wished to come along in the aftermath of the previous week's terror attack at the Manchester Arena.

At around the same time that Susan was sharing this news online, I was with the 'other' Susan – Susan Iacovou – back at the Percy Street training venue, where things were well underway in delivering training to the third cohort of volunteers. I was also being interviewed by BBC North West at the time, after they had come to visit us to see things in action. I left the training centre quite late that afternoon and was excited to head across to the pop-up centre on Tib Street for the first time since we'd opened.

At 4.45pm, I had declared on social media that an angel had walked into my life. I hadn't initially known who he was, but my eyes were drawn to a certain gentleman straight away as he wandered around the centre, taking in the unfurnished surroundings and gathering information from our team about what we were doing. A few minutes prior to the angel walking in I had been saying to my team that we needed somehow to be able to divide up our space into workable areas. I knew in my head exactly what I wanted it to look like: a group space in that corner, a couple of one-to-one rooms in that corner, a media centre over there by the window (as we were drawing a lot of press interest), an office space at the back and a lounge area at the entrance to welcome people in for a free hot or cold drink if all they wanted was a safe place to sit, knowing that there was a professional on site if needed. Seeming satisfied, the gentleman went to leave. Something about the situation told me to stop him and to encourage him to offer something of his feelings in the hope that we could help him. It transpired that this gentleman had not been directly affected in any way by the attack, but that he was *a shopfitter* who was merely visiting the city in a bid to seek work and a new place to live. A shopfitter! I mean, what's that all about? My angel!

My angel's expertise as a shopfitter was exactly what we needed, sitting here in our unfurnished space. I told him that I needed him to help me and I needed him to do it now!

Given the fact that my new friend was from Nottingham and had no real ties to Manchester, he agreed to help me. I explained to him that I don't have any materials. "Neither have I," he answered. "I don't have any tools," he proclaimed.

"Neither have I," I replied. So between us we did not have any tools or materials to carry out any kind of work on the level required, but my angel told me not to worry and to come promptly with him. He would sort it! So within 45 minutes, this angel (real name Rob Atlas) and I were in a city centre branch of B&Q, telling our story to the person on the customer service desk. Rob the Angel had become so immersed in the Heads Up project that I had briefed him on, that when he spoke, he referred to our charity as though he had been involved forever. The staff and the manager at B&Q were incredibly supportive in helping us out by offering us a discretionary manager's discount, and so Rob began touring the shop floor to fill our trollies.

At 6.05pm, with trollies loaded, we found ourselves at the checkout and were pleased to take advantage of the substantial discount from the B&Q store manager. I handed over my personal credit card. Our trollies were loaded with materials, but we still had no equipment with which to work. This would be sure to carry an even bigger expense than the materials. This is where the store manager was amazing once more, and asked, with a wink in his eye, if we were familiar with B&Q policy. We weren't. And so he continued to reveal to us that if we bought the equipment and 'didn't like it', then we could just bring it back... Thank you, B&Q. In the space of two hours, I had met the two most beautiful strangers.

Just before I could feel too happy about things, it hit me that Rob and I had no way at all of getting all of this stuff back to Tib Street, seeing as we'd ventured here empty-handed on the bus! Whether it was naivety, trust or just sheer belief in human goodness, I took Rob's word for it that he would 'sort it', and so I left things with him as I headed to my next urgent appointment.

I was expecting, given the speed of things so far, that the work fitting out the shop would likely be carried out the next day – providing that Rob, a man I had only just met, hadn't done a runner with all the loot that I had just paid for on my own credit card. In fact, Rob's actions couldn't have been further from that scenario. He had somehow arranged the pick-up of our haul of shopfitting materials and equipment and arranged for it all to be transported straight away to Tib Street, so that he could get started immediately on the work. Rob stayed so late that night and was so keen to get cracking early the next morning, that he slept at the venue overnight. He later told me that the only reason he stopped working wasn't in fact to sleep, but because a resident in one of the flats above our shop had complained about the noise. Up until then, it hadn't even occurred to me that people lived on that road. Having said that, it also hadn't occurred to me that a man I had only just met, who had no ties to me whatsoever, would be voluntarily giving his blood, sweat and tears to carry out the mammoth task of fitting our shop front at midnight on a Bank Holiday Monday. When the volunteers arrived the next day, Rob was already working, and he continued to do so until long after the volunteers had left that evening.

Let's just remember that Rob didn't live in Manchester, nor did he have any real link to the city except for the fact that he wanted to move there if he could find a job as a shopfitter. What he'd found instead, was a monumental shopfitting project that gave him no money, and a bed for the night surrounded by sawdust and bare walls. Rob had been due to go back to Nottingham that Monday night, but after having taken a short detour to B&Q, he didn't leave Manchester for the next month. Instead, Rob stayed on and became one of our biggest supporting volunteers. I will never be able to thank him enough for effectively putting his life on hold and moving away from home to support us. Like I said, an angel walked into my life that day.

On the Wednesday that week, the final day of the month, the new Lord Mayor of Manchester, Councillor Eddie Newman, called my friend Maurice. He wanted to come and see us at what was now being colloquially called 'MA17'. The councillor was new in post and was enthusiastic about getting out and about in his community. I viewed the prospect of a mayoral visit as official public recognition, and as an unofficial opening, of sorts. We were truly up and running.

Our mode of operation for the support centre wasn't just about waiting for people to come in to see us. Each day, as per a rota we had put together, we would send groups out into the city centre – primarily St Ann's Square – to talk to members of the public. Our 'field teams' went out each day in all weathers. They gave out leaflets to invite people to the centre, and they spoke to local people in a bid to help them, reassure them and provide a sense of wellbeing. We also used the field teams as a way of spreading the word of our telephone helpline, which we'd set up for those people who perhaps didn't feel comfortable attending a shared space to talk through the events that had so tragically affected our community. The helpline was manned, naturally, by our wonderful volunteers.

Logistically, everything was running smoothly, and Maurice had put programmes in place to ensure that all volunteers had a role, and that these were ever-changing on a rota to give everyone the chance to get involved at all levels. It really was all about teamwork.

Thursday 1 June. The start of a new month, and the middle of one of the busiest weeks I'd experienced in a long time. It was about to get a lot busier, however, as a frantic Susan approached me. "I have good news and bad news," she said. "The good news is that Buckingham Palace have just called us."

"Fantastic," I said. "And the bad news is?" I asked in trepidation.

"That I didn't answer the phone in time," she answered me. "They had left a voicemail though," she quickly reassured me. "Unfortunately," she continued excitedly, "I deleted the message." We had to see the funny side, and of course there was always the possibility that the call was a hoax. On the off-chance that the call was legit, Susan did what she could to track down a number for the Palace, in the hope that whichever staff member had called would have left a note on a system somewhere to allow her message to be passed through their detailed communication web. She did what I think anyone would have done when making such a call, and ventured forward with a tentative, "Hi, this is going to sound ridiculous, but…" Luckily, the representative at the Palace whom Susan had managed to connect with was more than helpful. She had recognition of the name and was able to pass her through to the appropriate person. Such a saving grace to have a memorable name like Iacovou!

The reason for the phone call from Buckingham Palace was to inform us that Prince William would be visiting Manchester the following day to pay his respects after the attack on the arena. As part of his visit, he wanted to meet with key people who had been of help and support to the victims, their families and the wider community. We were of course honoured and delighted to have been included in that group, and immediately said yes to whatever the Prince's aides needed us to do. As part of the plan, we were given strict confidential orders regarding a meet-up at Manchester Cathedral. We were asked to wear a uniform or unifying 'dress' to show which group or service we belonged to. Our uniform was a little less traditional than those of our counterparts at the gathering. The Heads Up CIO team were always identified by bright orange T-shirts. Susan and I wore our T-shirts with pride on the day of the royal meet, and I also had one of the shirts boxed up, as I wanted to give it as a gift to Prince William when I met him.

The T-shirts had been a donation from a community interest company called Emerging Futures, who were also the people behind the provision of the Percy Street training venue. It was another example of how the individuals and organisations of the North West were pulling together to help us help those affected by the attack on the City of Manchester. The colour of the T-shirts was known and referred to as 'safety orange', which I thought was an appropriate choice. This particular hue is said to set things apart from their surroundings and so is easily spotted and identifiable, which is what we needed our volunteers to be – a beacon of hope, a light at the end of the tunnel, sunlight on the horizon from what had been a dark day in the city. Apparently, this 'safety' shade of orange was deemed in industry to be so identifiable due to its 'contrast with the azure sky'. Obviously, these people have never been to Manchester!

This bright shade of orange was also a colour that was prevalent in the programme administered by Dr Farchi at Tel-Hai College, where, of course, I had taken my inspiration for the work of Heads Up CIO. Utilising the colour in my own programme was my homage to the doctor and his work. It really was the perfect colour, and one that attracted people to ask us about the T-shirts. Believe it or not, the shirts weren't influenced in any way by a contractual term for easyJet donating the tickets to fly our trainers over from Israel!

On Friday 2 June, Susan and I donned our T-shirts and met with Prince William's personal secretary at

Manchester Cathedral for a briefing. We were politely asked not to take photos during the session, though were told that we would be more than welcome to use the official ones that would be taken as part of the meet. As all the invited guests mingled together and praised each other for the efforts they had shown in supporting the people of Manchester both at the time and in the aftermath of the attack, it became apparent that there was a significant worry permeating the atmosphere... do we bow, curtsy, or shake hands with the Prince? We were told that Prince William is very informal when he meets people, and we shouldn't worry about anything like that. A polite but firm handshake would appeal to him rather than a bow.

As we waited excitedly, I took in just how wonderful were these people who surrounded me... we had people from the British Red Cross and St John Ambulance, who had administered essential aid on the night, a local taxi company who had taken people to safety, and members of staff from Northern Rail who had acted quickly and efficiently given their proximity to the attack... You will have to forgive me for not listing everybody, but I was truly taken aback by these amazing people who had given more help than I think they will ever quite realise. I was humbled to be a part of this small and privileged group.

Prince William arrived and engaged politely and enthusiastically with everyone. Although I had initially never wanted to put myself forward as a man of religion, I introduced myself as a rabbi, as this was how the media had been presenting me. The Prince asked about the T-shirts and read the print on the front aloud:

National Emergency Response, Resilience and Treatment Programme for Stress and Trauma. I told Prince William all about the background to the project and our unique protocols. Susan was cheeky and told him that our charity didn't have a patron. She used it as an in-road to hint if it was possible for him to take on that role... His response was, "There are means and there are ways." It wasn't a 'no', so I'm still hopeful.

Earlier that day, we had been told that the charity would be getting a donation of bunnies to the centre on Tib Street. In my royal haze, I didn't really have chance to process that information fully. To be honest, we had been getting all sorts donated and delivered, such as furniture, food and office supplies. The good people of Manchester supported us fully, and we had everything we needed to run our essential programme from our venue and out in the field. A box of cuddly toy bunnies would be strange, but I assumed there was logic to it from the point of view of the person donating them.

I was told that the lady from Prestwich – named Carin Stein Travers – would be dropping the stuffed animals off in a car outside the venue, as there was nowhere to park on the street. It would be a relatively straightforward exchange and I was looking forward to seeing any visiting children playing with the toys whilst their parents talked with our volunteers. Well, imagine my surprise when the cuddly toys in the box I had handed to me started moving! Carin zipped away in the car, telling me she'd be back after she'd parked up, so I spent the next five minutes, ironically, in shock! Well, at least I was in the right place for such a state!

When our new friend returned, she told me that the bunnies were for therapy, and that people could use them to stroke and interact with as a way to get their thoughts out. I panicked. Where would they sleep? What would they eat? What would happen to the poo? Thankfully, Carin told me that she would be staying with the bunnies each day and would take them home after they had 'served their purpose'. Well, the bunnies became a big hit, and I remember police officers just as much as children fussing over and petting the bunnies before they spoke with us. I have such respect for such a therapeutic approach and attraction, and I must thank Carin immensely for taking me from Buckingham Palace to bunny madness in the space of just a few hours.

During this busy week, easyJet had delivered on their promise, in quite the most literal form. We had welcomed the arrival of Judith Barr-Hay Kovatch on 30 May. Her speciality was in two areas. One was running the support centres in Israel for those working at centres like ours, where she very much 'helped the helpers' as part of a peer-to-peer support protocol. She was a real asset in facilitating how our volunteers could help each other. Additionally, Judith was also an expert in operational mobile units, which we were venturing out to utilise. A lady named Wendy Radnan from the Jewish community in Manchester gave her accommodation, and almost from the hour of her arrival, Judith really threw herself into everything we were doing at Heads Up CIO. She supervised, but she also got stuck in. She trained the helpers, but she also helped people directly.

Such intensive support from all those involved with Heads Up CIO proved to be of incredible help as we scrambled together to see how we might provide support at the then recently announced 'One Love' benefit concert. The event had been put together by singer, Ariana Grande, who, as you may know, was performing her concert at the Manchester Arena on the night it was targeted by a suicide bomber. We took interest in Ariana's somewhat controversial decision, but we wanted and needed to be there at the benefit concert to support all of those in attendance. We realised that people going to the concert would be frightened and that the event, to be held at Manchester's famous Old Trafford Cricket Ground, would be a potential target for a further attack. We wanted to get among the crowds outside as they waited to go in, reassuring them in any way we could. A presence of a psycho-trauma emergency response unit such as ours was a historical first in terms of pre-emptive and preventative measures. We couldn't just turn up outside, though. We would have to go through proper channels.

To get everything arranged, we needed a lady called Jo Almond. Jo had been put forward by Dr Sandi Mann as somebody who was efficient and who would get things done for us – whatever we needed. She came across as not only someone who got things done, but someone who got straight to the point, and I liked that. I told Jo about the One Love concert that would be taking place later that week on Sunday 4 June. Everything she wrote down, happened. She made effective contact with Greater Manchester Police and Trafford Council, who were the authorities behind the planning of the concert. Such a communication task hadn't been easy, as such authorities were obviously having to deal with a lot in terms of the concert – with or without the potential threat of a repeat terrorist attack.

The day of One Love was to be my first 'in the field' activity that wasn't geared towards the pop-up support centre. I wanted to put in place safety and communication methods for my team, and I felt a huge sense of responsibility to each one of them. My duty was to them as theirs was to the people at the concert. I gave each of our volunteers a number, 1–30, so that it was easy to count everyone being there. They shouted out their number at set times so that we could note by silence if anyone was missing. I also utilised communication via WhatsApp, the social media messaging app. I encouraged the team to work in pairs to give peer responsibility and a sense of support. Everyone was also instructed that they must always be able to see me, so I would base myself at the nucleus of a radius around the outside of the ground. With these systems in place, we would be able to congregate quickly if we needed to.

The team had done all they could in the aftermath of a traumatic event. Now, they would need to be on standby 'in the moment' in case it happened again.

As part of the team that day, I took a friend and personal trainer of mine, Ryan Crooks – a former semi-pro boxer and member of security staff of the nightclubs of Manchester – to join in with our efforts. I felt that an element of personal security would add further weight to what we were doing. Ryan was well known in the city, and he was both recognised and respected, so he was a conduit for safety. I also wanted to take my friend Jeff

Kwartz, who is a surgeon, and would therefore contribute an additional medical facet within our network.

On the day, we attracted familiar members of the press who were keen to speak with us again, having documented our work so far already. Amid talking with them, we spoke with as many people as possible in the queues at the gates of the concert. Parents were more anxious than their children and young people, and we had anticipated this. Ariana Grande's fanbase was predominantly children and young people, and such a demographic sadly accounted for a large number of those whose lives were taken in the previous month's attack. There was palpable tension amid the excitement, and so it made me feel positive that we could at least support if not intervene with these people as such. We didn't want anyone to feel alone, which sounds ridiculous when you see a crowd so big. Fear can enhance the sense of loneliness, however, and this loneliness can breed more fear. Our presence, I had hoped, would be a sense of comfort.

The event was a complete success. Ariana brought everyone together, and music began, slowly, to heal a lot of the wounds created less than two weeks earlier. Money was raised by the concert to support those directly affected and their families, and hope was shone across the world from our wonderful city. As a group, the volunteers at Heads Up CIO became crystallised in our work, our ethos and our relationship with each other. Should we have needed to, we could work together again for the good of the community.

Little did we know just how soon we would be needed.

Rob 'The Angel' in B&Q

'The Group Room'

Entrance to support centre

The media centre

The bunnies

Ariana Grande concert 'One Love'

Heads Up responders
with Police

Meeting HRH
Prince William

Ryan - Head of Security & Jo - gets things done!

Lord Mayor of Manchester

DOV ON... EXPERIENCE IN THE MILITARY

My experience and opinion of the military will not be the same as everyone else's. It depends on *how* you are involved, to what *level* you are involved, and indeed *where* you are involved. I allude several times in this book to the fact that I feel my experience of the military is that it is exceptional in its approach to leadership and its support for anyone under its charge or care. It certainly shaped who I am today, and much of the content you will read about in this book.

There are military schools and training academies worldwide, and they are all similar in terms of their DNA – their strategy, their tactics, their operations. There are differences, though. For example, prior to joining the military myself, I was physically unfit and in no way athletic. Whilst some military schools may require a base level for entry, I'm confident that I wouldn't have achieved this standard at those locations! They say that the army creates soldiers, and in my case, this was very much what needed to be done, as I was in no way the kind of physical specimen that you would associate with being a solider, never mind one fit for combat. In addition, at the age of 21, I was considered 'old', and I didn't help my case in being classed as more than just a 'casual' smoker. The army would have its work cut out for it with me, but then, isn't that what good training and leadership should be about – adding value?

Although entering the military at a time where conflict was very much a real prospect, I was very motivated. My military experience didn't just teach me to act, it taught me to think. It taught me about intelligence and it encouraged me to use my brain as well as my body. You learn to follow orders, but you also learn to lead. What's more, you are trained to the level above the one you are serving at, owing to the preparedness of taking over from your leader should anything happen to them. You hope it won't, but it can, and you need to be ready. It was an active army, after all.

Having loved my role within the army and wanting to develop, I applied for an elite unit within operations, whereby all applicants were sent on an intensive week-long selection programme of survival. It was physical, and it was mental in terms of the challenges we would face, and I would learn that we were not being judged on who came through at the end, but rather on *how* we came through along the way. It was a real opportunity to show leadership and teamwork, rather than a chance to adopt a mentality of every man for themselves and survival at all costs.

Last man standing is no leadership at all.

A VIEW FROM
THE BRIDGE

The day before the One Love concert, there had been a further terrorist attack on the UK. This time, the attack was in London, and the terrorists had targeted two popular areas with tourists and residents alike, in the form of the iconic London Bridge and the famous Borough Market.

The attackers at both sites had worn belts laden with what turned out to be fake explosives, but this sight will have been more than enough to further heighten the terror experienced by innocent civilians, when a van mounted the busy pavement on the bridge, and people were attacked with knives whilst enjoying their evening out in the market. Eight people died in that act of terrorism that night, and 48 were injured. The attack was brought to a halt with police officers shooting the attackers dead on sight. It seemed to mark a quick end to such a monumental attack, but the entire event seemed to seep painfully into the next few days, as bodies were still being found in the aftermath, presumably after people had been knocked – or perhaps even willingly jumped – into the river below the bridge after the van mounted the pavement.

It was imperative that we dealt with the Ariana Grande concert first, but I knew that soon after, our team at Heads Up CIO would need to get down to London.

I had spoken with all members of our newly-formed team regarding the question of who would be willing and able to make the journey with me. I knew that it was a big ask, for many reasons.

Around this time, I was in contact with a high-profile media adviser, who shall remain nameless, through my cousin, Brian McCallum, who is also a trustee of Heads Up CIO. The adviser had always joked that his job was either to get people into the public eye, or to keep people out of it. Given the nature of his work, he had a lot of government and political-based clients, as you can imagine. When I called him to ask for his opinion regarding my proposed actions, his advice to me was a very curt, "Don't come to London." He qualified this statement by reminding me that the General Election was coming up the following Thursday, and therefore, the Government would be wanting to 'clean things up' and move on quickly from the weekend's events. Whereas back in Manchester, the arena – as the centre of the attack – went on to be closed for several months, London, it would seem, would not be operating like that and would not be dwelling on giving the attack more focus than it had already gained. There are many views on this, and it is not my place to judge regarding whether this is the right way or wrong way to deal with such events, but I will say that I can see both sides. Regardless, the conversation had thrown me off balance. I took the initial approach that my media colleague was right, and that I shouldn't travel to London.

Having said all of this, my feelings centred around a wavering rather than a firm decision, and this was because I felt uneasy thinking that I may be dragging my team of volunteers into something potentially political. I really didn't want anybody to get caught up in anything like that. However, on a personal and professional level, I strongly and wholly felt that our organisation would be truly needed right now, no matter how badly it could have affected our reputation. It wasn't about us, so I decided to get a second opinion, and called on my very good friend Shai, from SQR Security, with whom I had delivered corporate resilience training some months earlier. Shai was – and still is – hugely supportive of all that I do and had always offered any resources that he could to support Heads Up CIO. I told Shai about my original plan to journey to London, and my indecision regarding the advice I'd already been given. Put simply, Shai asked me if I'd lost my mind. Shai is what we'd call a typical mission-oriented person. He was adamant that I needed to get down to London with my team as soon as possible, as my whole mission had been based precisely on what was going on right now – helping those in need following a traumatic event. It didn't matter who, what or why when it came to politics – I had to get down there, otherwise, what was the point in doing what we were doing? Shai gave me confidence as well as reason, and I announced to the group that the London visit was a definite go!

Whilst down in the capital, I wanted to take an opportunity to train up more volunteers for our cause, just as we had done in Manchester. Shai would provide the training facilities, Professor Yori Gidron would join us once more to lead training, and BA would be the airline to help us immensely by flying him across from his post in Belgium. I will always be so appreciative to easyJet for being our initial airline, but on this occasion, sadly Brussels to any of the London airports wasn't a route they operated.

It was very important for me to get our team to London within 72 hours of the attack having taken place, as our unique intervention protocols operate best within this timeframe. Owing to our less than fledgling status at the time of the attack in Manchester, we'd missed that window. This time, however, we were properly established in all senses. Although I stand by the fact that our work in Manchester had been crucial, I knew that we could do even more in London given how quickly we would be able to engage in the aftermath. It's an arbitrary figure really, but theory and practice would suggest that supporting people within 72 hours of psychological shock or an acute stress reaction in a life-threatening situation really is the most effective. In my opinion, the quicker you can help somebody, the better.

On the Monday following the attack on the nation's capital, at 3.14pm, I posted a status update on our Facebook page. It advertised free training at London North Business Park, home of SQR Security, for mental health professionals for that coming Wednesday morning. Recruitment began.

At 23.09 that night, I was busy organising the set-up of two pop-up support centres via the acceptance and commitment therapy (ACT) community. An ACT colleague called Tien Kuei had not only generously helped arrange these, she also wanted to go through the training herself. Locations for the centres were at London Philharmonia (not Philharmonic) Orchestra rehearsal rooms in Southwark, and at a business centre called Longcroft House, which was based near the city's famous Spitalfields Market. As it turned out, we used those locations as a base for our work, but we ended up providing all our support out at 'Ground Zero', so to speak.

In terms of getting ourselves down to London in the first place, only five people signed up from our original Manchester group – including me. I knew it would be a big ask to get a higher number, as not only would we need people to leave their homes, jobs and families at short notice for the best part of a week, but also it was a much more daunting task ahead at being involved so closely in the aftermath of such a significant terror attack. The five recruited volunteers ended up being just the four of us: Catherine Russel, Roz Ewart, Damien Mayoh and me. The original fifth was a lady called Coralie Hobson, and although she was unable to go to London at the last minute, she was instrumental in enabling the rest of the team to get down there in the first place. She worked tirelessly to sort arrangements and deals for transport and accommodation so that we could leave as soon as possible. Her (now) late father, nicknamed Poppa Bear, made a very generous £200 donation to fund the trip (our first ever money donation), having seen how important our work was to his daughter. Coralie also secured a donation of vouchers from Merseyrail, based in her home city of Liverpool, whereby we could exchange the rail vouchers over in Manchester to travel direct to London on Virgin Trains. I was completely taken aback by Merseyrail's gesture for essentially funding a trip we would take outside of their network. I think it's important to mention here that we had asked Virgin directly if they would fund the travel, and they would not. Coralie's partner, Colin, even drove across from Liverpool to Manchester so that he could place the vouchers quickly and safely in our hands. It seemed that in having lost Coralie from our onsite team, we had gained the support of most of her family back up at home.

Coralie was also trying to organise accommodation for us upon our arrival, but it seemed that people were not getting back to her. We were due to be leaving on the train at 15.35 on the Tuesday, and with accommodation still very uncertain, it became clear to me that we were very fortunate that Coralie would be staying 'back at base' rather than having to immerse her time and talents in field work with the rest of us. Ultimately, however, Coralie ended up using her own money to book some accommodation for the group and did so via the popular Airbnb website. I was appreciative of her gesture but very upset with Coralie for putting her hand in her own pocket. Charity is not about you having to do everything yourself, but about drawing on a group and having lots of people pull together. Regardless, I was very grateful for what she had done.

After arriving in London by train, we made our way to the accommodation that Coralie had booked over in Marble Arch. We were tired and wanted to get settled in, but more importantly, we wanted to get out there among the people of the city. Our plans to get straight out onto the streets were somewhat halted, however, because one of the bedrooms in our apartment had a very prominent leak. Coralie contacted the landlord and he said he'd get it all repaired. She asked for him also to fix the gas cooker, which it transpired was also broken.

With all this getting taken care of while we were out, I didn't want to take the team straight to London Bridge. I wanted a softer landing for the sake of my team's wellbeing, and, therefore, our first intervention took place on the busy shopping thoroughfare of Oxford Street. We got in amongst the shoppers and told them all about how we worked and what we were doing. We also spoke to people working in the district, such as those out driving taxi bikes. In all the conversations we had with that group, there seemed to be conflicting stories. Some people reported how business was fine, whilst others said there had been a negative effect since the attack. Some people had the British attitude of 'stiff upper lip', whilst others were happy to let their guard down and explain in heartfelt detail the impact that things had on them because of the attack. It became clear that what we were doing at this location wasn't just about intervention or providing treatment of any sort; it was also about being a friendly face, a comforting shoulder and a listening ear.

The next group of people we approached was a group of teenagers. They told us that they were on the bridge at the actual time of the attack. They were visiting England on a trip over from their school in Scandinavia. They said that they didn't really want to talk about the events, but they did say how their school had offered them psychological help in the aftermath. It was clear that these kids were still visibly shaken from everything that had gone on, but I was heartened to hear about how they were being supported.

After these initial interactions had taken place, I encouraged our team to disperse and go off on their own. It can be hard to talk to people in the street, regardless of intention, but I think I'm right in saying that we all met interesting people that day and heard emotive and in-the-moment stories from people who were actively there during the attacks on the bridge and at the market only a few hours ago. We spoke with people from different races, cultures and religions, and I started up a Facebook Live 'story' to showcase our work across social media and to bring together the nation as best we could in our own small way. We generated a lot of comments and expressions of further interest from people wanting to join our campaign, and so from this we directed them to sign up to volunteer.

The weather turned cold and wet and we were exhausted from a physically and mentally tiring day. On top of this, we needed to move out of our apartment as the landlord was busy arranging repairs on the one we had initially booked. Once at the new location, we ate, we settled, we slept, and then headed out the next morning to London Bridge.

Though our team was much smaller this time, I gave our volunteers the same briefing as the one I had given at the One Love concert – everybody stays in pairs and in sight of me. My primary concern, as always, was the safety and stability of my team. I added the instruction that I wanted everybody to sense the tone of the atmosphere and gauge how people were feeling before reacting appropriately. I wanted our team to find out what people were talking about, and I wanted our people to make their presence felt in those conversations. It wasn't only about going in there and saving lives; it was just about being there.

London Bridge that day was filled with people, as you would expect, and the pavements were covered in flowers of tribute. There was a message wall filled with post-it notes of love and remembrance, marking the exact location of the point of impact where the van driven by the attackers mounted the kerb causing mass casualties. Though the bridge was as busy as it ever was, there was a solemn atmosphere. Considering how recent the attack was, it was almost surprising to witness the lack of hysteria. I don't think it was lost on anybody, however, that there was still a person lost or, if you prefer, unaccounted for, following on from the attack several days earlier. This visibly and audibly hung over the city's beloved landmark that day.

Whilst we were at the bridge, several members of the police approached us, presumably being drawn to our bright orange T-shirts. They were probably also more than a little intrigued by the title of 'Chief' emblazoned on my big 'safety orange' jacket. This title was little to do with megalomania, I can assure you, but one that I believed authorities and agencies would respect if they could see that there was a distinguished person in charge of an organised group. The attitude of the police officers who approached us surprised me, as rather than question our presence or 'move us on', they opened up to us emotionally. After all, the attack had taken place on their patch, so to speak, a patch where people had lost their lives and were living in fear. It transpired, too, that they had colleagues who had been injured in the attack. These events really do affect everybody on some level.

Our time on the bridge proved very tough, and the team went through a small crisis. One of our members said they 'couldn't do it anymore', so I regrouped with all of them together away from the action to talk. It seemed that from a cultural point of view, they felt that offering help in a public and highly exposed place was different from serving in a pop-up centre or in a generic public space whereby no attack had physically taken place, as with the gatherings at St Ann's Square in Manchester. My team members were increasingly uncomfortable and overwhelmed the more they listened to stories and the more of the atmosphere they soaked up in the aftermath. This was of course completely natural, but it needed to be dealt with, and I was happy that they had expressed their feelings. I reminded them how much they were needed, and how proud I was that all they had trained for was now being actively deployed in the exact scenario it was designed for. Peer-to-peer support was in action, because if you can't help your team, then they can't help anyone else. We carried out our peer-to-peer protocol and discussed our situation and talked about our 'how and why'. I reassured them and expressed that I knew it was unpleasant, but that their work wasn't a personal interaction but a professional duty. It wasn't going to be comfortable, but empathy rarely is. The team was remotivated and gladly re-entered the bridge.

Earlier that morning, the training had taken place for the London-based volunteers wanting to sign up to our Heads Up CIO projects. One of the volunteers, a lady called Amanda Marks, was so keen to get started that she generously collected our trainer, Yori, from the airport on her way across London. Twenty people had signed up to the training, which was a fantastic turnout considering the short notice. Shai's classroom at his offices wasn't big enough, so he hired another one for us to relocate to, all at his own expense. Although the initial venue wasn't quite big enough, the response from volunteers wanting to sign up was less than I would have liked, if I'm honest. However, there will have been reasons for this. London is one of the busiest capital cities in the world, and it's fairly well renowned for being less of a community, and more of a gathering of people present in their own worlds. Sadly, in living in one of the world's most high-profile cities, exposure to terrorist threat and events is a very real presence in people's lives. I could completely understand that people at this time would be fractious, insular, and keen to keep their heads down and just keep moving forward.

Carin Stein Travers, our bunny benefactor, had become a good friend to the cause since she and 20 rabbits bounded into our lives a week earlier, and she had arranged with her sister-in-law in North London for food to be provided and delivered to our training sessions. The sister-in-law, Susan, was a big part of the Jewish community and so took it upon herself to also sort meals for our field team on each of the days we resided in the city. I was absolutely taken aback on that first day of training, seeing all the food get delivered in taxis. Total strangers helping total strangers – the power of people helping people. It was a lovely morning of training and togetherness.

Out of the 20 volunteers who trained with us that morning, only two wanted to come along and help out for the rest of the day on site at Ground Zero. This, of course, was their decision, and I understood the short notice, but I was a little disappointed. Despite the lack of sign-up after the event, the day went well in terms of what we had set out to do. It was cathartic and there was clarity.

Tired, cold and hungry, our team got the bus back to our original apartment, which had since had all the repairs carried out. We were drained, and our brains were frazzled, but what snapped us back into reality was the potent smell of gas emanating from our apartment as we approached it on the walk up from the bus stop. Immediately, we phoned Coralie to get her up to speed so that she could act on this problem for us by notifying the landlord. Coralie advised us that, in the meantime, we needed to call the police and the gas board to report this potentially explosive incident. As it turned out, the police naturally had other things to worry about, but the gas board were quick to turn up, and it was good that they did, because the landlord didn't turn up until much later.

An inspection at around 10pm showed that although the faulty gas cooker had been fixed, the job had been botched, and that was what was causing the dangerous and worrying gas leak. The landlord was only in his early twenties and had been clearly dragged out of a nightclub or similar to come back to the apartment, girlfriend in tow. He looked bewildered and out of his depth. In the meantime, Coralie was trying hard to get us alternative accommodation, but to be fair, the landlord really did step up to try to do the same. By now, it was close to midnight, but he found us a place to stay in Knightsbridge. Whilst we travelled there, Coralie called to say that she had managed to book a Hilton hotel, and that she had secured a £12k reduction on the bill! You can guess my question… *"How much was the accommodation originally billed as?!"* I took the decision that an apartment would be much more suitable than a hotel, as it would help to keep our group functioning together. In addition, seeing as the landlord was so worried about the rating we'd be leaving for him on Airbnb, he refunded Coralie's money that she had already laid out, and gave us the Harrod's adjacent apartment for free. He told us that he was incredibly sorry for all that had gone on and hoped that his gesture would help us to leave a favourable rating for him. Ethically, this didn't sit well with me, so we didn't leave a rating at all – which I think will have spoken volumes.

I didn't think it was possible to feel more drained right now, but I was to be surprised. As we debriefed on the day's events, it was to be confirmed that a body had been found and identified just yards from where we had been working earlier that day. It was the body of Xavier Thomas, the Frenchman previously unaccounted for from the night of the attack.

Heads Up volunteers at Borough Market

Entrance closed to Borough Market

On the way to London Bridge

On the bridge

Words cannot express the amount of gratitude that I have for everyone involved in MA17 and LB17. I can honestly say that I have met the most extraordinary people that I have ever met in my life in the last 10 days. You have been creative, enthusiastic, motivated, independent, empowered, patient, flexible and have taken initiatives that have contributed to a paradigm shift - a shift to living and doing valued action of resilience in the face of murderous, destructive behaviour. You have made a choice NOT to participate in this war but to drop the rope and do something useful that will strengthen yourselves and others. What I witnessed in Manchester and London was none other than life-saving moments. We are just at the beginning of a Resilience Revolution where together we will stand in the face of adversity to make this world a nurturing and healthier place. Thank you for believing in this and for your continued support and for accompanying me on this journey. Enjoy the rest, for there is much work still to be done. Bvracha and love, Dov.

Facebook status from Dov

DOV ON... TERRORISM

Though the word has a powerful effect and has the capacity to instil fear, it's my view that terrorism represents nothing more than bullying. Yes, it's large scale, but it's bullying nonetheless in the fact that it is based in cowardice. Terrorists know what they want, but as they cannot gain it through respect, they will get it however they can through the most destructive and painful means, which is nearly always as desired as any other commodity they seek. Their chosen currency is one of fear.

Terrorists will describe themselves as soldiers, which I find offensive when we think of the good work done by military people across the world. The biggest lesson I learned as a solider was how to deal with enemies of any kind, and that includes terrorists. What I always found fascinating was that, as soldiers, we were never taught the name of our enemy, even when we were surrounded by them. When we were training, we took part in war games with live ammunition, so that everything was real and ready, and so that we could learn to exercise care in what we were doing and to limit mistakes, rather than to foster a blanket approach to an attack. Whether real or simulated, however, we never named the enemy. We weren't fighting people, we were fighting a force and defending our families and our nation. Through this approach, we came out of combat without having learned to hate a group of people, a demographic, or a society.

The after-effects of war can have drastic consequences for soldiers in the form of PTSD, and so adding hatred into that mix is as unhealthy as it is unhelpful. As a soldier, you are of course trained to kill, but to get things into perspective, you are trained firstly to defend. A true military may train you in the ability to kill, but they do not teach you to do it proactively or as a first response. Your job as a soldier is to neutralise a threat. Therefore I can never view a terrorist as being a soldier. If you can keep the peace, then you should.

Terrorism is bullying that is used to prove a point. It's an attempt to break someone both physically and mentally, either through a violent act or through the wake of its impact in what it leaves behind. In terms of 'recruiting' to this regime, terrorists are training humans to hate. Sadly, once you train someone to hate, you can get them to do almost anything at all.

WAR ROOMS

We were approaching the end of our second week of provision as a recognised organisation, and Heads Up CIO were operating on a dual-front mission, working effectively in both Manchester and now in London. Maurice was back in Manchester keeping us running logistically with the pop-up centre on Tib Street and our field team out and about in the city centre and surrounding areas, and Coralie was continuing to prove a great resource to support me in running things down at the other end of the country in London.

Although I trusted Maurice completely, it wasn't lost on me that it was very much my responsibility to keep morale high in both locations, and to demonstrate clear leadership across the scope of the organisation. In being 200 miles away from Manchester, where it all began, this was very difficult. It would come to light that my absence was very much felt back in my home city, not because the team physically needed me, but because they *believed* that they did. From what I came to learn afterwards, without me as their leader present, faith and self-confidence in everyone's own ability to do the best possible job they could merely dropped. All our volunteers were working exceptionally hard on everything that they had been tasked and trained to do, but it's often very typical with new teams, which we were, to struggle in the absence of a leader. This was a strange concept for me and the culture I was brought up in; as I mentioned previously, I am not the kind of leader who micromanages or intrudes on their team's work and the intricate value and decision-making power that individuals bring, but it was clear that I should have been present with them, nonetheless. There is no one correct way to lead, but empowering and training others to lead is my style in all I do. I feel that this style of promoting leaders at all levels was an effective one in the circumstances we all found ourselves in, especially as our team were all giving so freely of their time, efforts and empathy.

In a less established setting, however, the team down in London was a new group going through a brand new experience, and so they really needed my full attention. Let me clarify: the *people* didn't need my full attention, as such, but the situation in which they all found themselves certainly did. As already mentioned, our intervention in the capital was at a much rawer time and location than our work in Manchester had been.

Torn between two cities, I of course tried incredibly hard to keep a presence in Manchester. The best way for me to do this was via messaging and imaging activity on WhatsApp, which I've already alluded to several times as being a fantastic group communication tool. This form of social media was, and still is, a great management resource for bringing people together. I could see who was active, and who had read messages. There's a lot to be said for the reassurance you feel in these fractious times when you know that a message you have sent has not only been received but also read.

Each arm of our organisation at Heads Up CIO had its own WhatsApp group, with MA17 (Manchester Arena) and LB17 (London Bridge) being the names of the two main operational groups. Those group chats served as 'war rooms', whereby vital information was shared, decisions were made and logistics were put into place. The people in MA17 were actively assisting me with the running of events and support up in Manchester. Our volunteer base there was strong and effective in terms of dealing with the public, which of course was our main aim, but another tier to this organisation was a layer of people who had contacts and resources to get things done for the good of the organisation. I made sure I was very active in that group, to make up for the fact that I couldn't be with them in person.

When it came to the volunteers out in the field in Manchester, doing our great work and spreading our positive messages, I didn't have a great deal of contact with them, I'm sad to say, as it just wasn't practical. However, they were managed effectively by Maurice, so I knew that they were in great hands.

In the WhatsApp group for 'war room' LB17, we had a few crossovers from the Manchester team. I wanted things to be as transparent as possible both within groups and indeed across them. Some information was privileged and only meant for certain eyes, but that was purely for the safety and wellbeing of my teams, as opposed to excluding anyone from information or attempting to construct a hierarchy through secrecy. In times like these, sometimes the less you know the happier you will be. For example, when the team in London had gone through their crisis of confidence on the second day of our trip out on the bridge, I did not share that event with anyone outside of the group. It was irrelevant, it would have been a breach of trust and it could have potentially shaken other members of the organisation.

As a team down in London, we were always at risk of things happening that might negatively affect us, such as getting split up from each other, facing another crisis of confidence, or, quite frighteningly, even being involved in another terrorist attack. I set up a third WhatsApp group and called it LB Scouts. This group included people based outside of the capital who I believed could and would help us should anything happen out in the field. This made complete sense, should the worst happen, and all the field team became indisposed or uncontactable.

Although my main source of communication was through the three WhatsApp groups, I made a point of also carrying on with the Facebook Live streams from our page whenever I could, so that followers old and new could tune in and catch up with what was happening at Heads Up CIO. Sometimes I think it's great for people to physically witness your active presence in some way, should you be absent in their physical company, so this video streaming was a great resource.

Two days into our work in London, my unofficial mentor, Dr Moshe Farchi, would be flying into Manchester at his own expense, to tie in with his availability from when I'd initially approached him about using his expertise to help with Heads Up CIO. I was devastated that I wouldn't get to see him or work with him and learn from him at this time, as well as welcome him to my wonderful home city, but I was delighted that he was true to his word about coming across to support us and deliver training as soon as he was free from other commitments.

Following a conversation I'd had the previous week, I was also at this time due to give a series of lectures to the psychology faculties at the University of Manchester and Manchester Metropolitan University. A lady called Louise Mansell had been keeping up with our work, so she took it upon herself to call me to see if there was any way that the former could become more prepared for the event of a future attack, if not more of a support in the aftermath of the most recent one. Both Louise and her husband were practising clinicians in Manchester, as well as Warren (her husband) serving as a lecturer to psychology students at the University of Manchester, and so they were excellent conduits for pushing the application of everything being taught to students in our city. Louise had told me during our initial phone call that as a high-profile and well-resourced institution in the city, the University of Manchester needed and wanted to be doing more for survivors of the Manchester Arena bombing. I naturally agreed to give a training lecture to their staff, but with me now being down in London, it made perfect sense for Dr Farchi to step in and replace me, both there and at Manchester Metropolitan, who were also on board. He was absolutely the best person to give the lectures, although I admit I was disappointed not to have been involved.

There's a popular opinion that high-profile institutions, perhaps such as universities, should do more in the aftermath of large-scale traumatic events, such as a terrorist attack. People call for human and physical resources to be allocated, but there are reasons why this often isn't feasible. In the UK, our response and care services act in line with guidelines published by NICE – the National Institute for Health and Care Excellence. In layman's terms, those guidelines suggest a 'watchful waiting' approach for at least a period of six weeks following a traumatic event – both in terms of events affecting whole communities, such as the attack at the arena, or circumstances affecting an individual, such as childbirth. Watchful waiting refers to the after-effects of an acute stress reaction (ASR) to the event or events witnessed. It is suggested that within six weeks, most people will either 'get over' or effectively 'deal with' the events and how they have been affected by them. Within that time, however, a fraction of people will develop what is known as an acute stress disorder (ASD), and then from this, a small percentage of people will develop and suffer from recognised post-traumatic stress disorder (PTSD). It is thought that from the original population of people involved in or affected by the event, only 5–15% of people will be diagnosed with PTSD, although there are of course certain circumstances where this can be significantly higher (up to more than 50%). It really doesn't sit well with me to use the term 'only' in this case, as it's my belief that this number is both significant and indeed still too high, because early or any intervention, as opposed to watching and waiting, could and would reduce this percentage dramatically. The NHS, however, are obliged to follow this guidance from NICE and so therefore, our professionals must wait until that six-week point. With other institutions guided by what the NHS suggest, you can understand their hesitance to run in and act differently.

In terms of an alternative to what NICE suggest in their guidelines, there seems to be somewhat of a void in terms of a common policy or co-ordinated package of support to even be advised of in the direct aftermath of traumatic events that affect communities on a large scale. As I've already alluded to earlier in this book, this is one of the reasons I was so adamant to set up an organisation such as Heads Up CIO. For a large majority of my life growing up in a country where early intervention for mental health is more abundant and accessible, it seemed wrong that such processes – or even just options – were not available in one of the most developed nations in the world – the UK. In Israel, the concept of watchful waiting just wouldn't be viewed as any kind of policy at all, never mind a preferred one. The thought is that it would leave us with a small percentage of people who could still be helped much earlier. Although the percentage may be small in terms of the community population, it's 100% for everyone who falls into that category.

In the case of PTSD, somebody suffering from the condition may go on to self-medicate if not given the appropriate intervention in the early stages, and this of course can lead to many more physical and mental health conditions. Furthermore, a lack of intervention is a false economy, as it opens a door that will be costly in the long run, for example with employers and family members of the person initially affected, who will go on to suffer the fall-out of a loved one or employee's condition. PTSD is an ordeal, and it's not just about the person suffering it. It seemed that Louise and the team she put me in contact with over at the university were to agree with this viewpoint and how the attack at the arena could be leading people down this path and wanted to do what they could to get involved.

Whilst Dr Farchi took on the lecture task with Louise, I had also arranged for him to deliver sessions to the staff at the King David Jewish Primary School in Manchester. This school was the one under the governance of my earlier contact, who I'd hoped would be able to let me access a network to support me with the initial set-up of Heads Up CIO. Rather than prove a 'way in' to the school, however, my contact was actively hesitant about my training taking place. I have no idea why. When teachers at the school got word of the offer, though, they lobbied to the governing body to get me involved. This training was to prove a very important pilot task for our organisation, as young people and schools are a key resource in working to filter through messages to the wider community. There is no more powerful tool than education, and no more powerful voice as that of our future generations to instil present cultural values and future cultural norms. I am also of the view that young people are absolutely the most responsive to work involving prevention and resilience. In this case, the pilot task was a huge success, and the teaching staff have asked for further training to take place.

As I write this, I am desperately flitting back and forth between my notes in my journals, messages on my phone, and news reports that were circulating at the time of all the events of which I speak. Please do forgive me if I get a specific day wrong; it's only just really hitting me how much was going on in such a short space of time. It was overwhelming at the time and reflecting on it now is still just as much of a flood of information and emotion.

With that in mind, let me draw you back to what was happening in London that week. I believe the day of the lecture at the University of Manchester was the Thursday following the attack on the bridge and in the market, and the day of the General Election. I remember being at our base near Spitalfields Market, and spending time there as we held a version of the pop-up support centre that had proved so popular and effective back in Manchester. On the Friday, we operated out of the base at the Philharmonia. On that day, we were off to an early start, and at 6.53am, I updated our Facebook page to promote both the pop-up centres and our work on the bridge. After a busy morning ended, we opted to visit the bridge one last time before making our train home to Manchester later that afternoon. On the way to the bridge, we walked through the Borough Market area. Although the market was closed for business, our walk through the area revealed many groups of people, all huddled together and openly speaking with each other about the events of the previous week. It was during this time that we spoke once again with members of the police with whom we had become familiar and indeed friendly, and after pleasantries were exchanged, they informed us that our presence would be very much needed on the bridge today.

As we made the short walk from the market to the bridge, the grief we witnessed as we walked up onto the imposing landmark became more and more palpable. It would transpire that this was in response to the news that had broken over the previous two days, whereby the body of missing Frenchman, Xavier Thomas, had been brought in from the River Thames below. The event was a clear reminder to everyone that even though the attackers had been shot on site, there was to be no such thing as a line drawn under the event where it could be marked as officially historic. The discovery of the body made the whole circumstance and the aftermath that much more fresh and painful, and you could both see and feel this on the bridge that day.

Whilst we were mindful of giving people the space they needed to grieve or simply just to take in the events as they wandered across the bridge, we were keen to speak with those who we could see were very much stationary, rather than those who were crossing from one side to the other as they may have done day in, day out. We spoke with a group of skateboarders, and to a woman who lived around the corner from where the attack had happened. It was an emotional exchange as she said that having spoken to Catherine – one of our LB17 team – she now felt safer to go back to her own home. A police officer opened up to us to state how he felt responsible in some way, given the fact that this whole event had happened on his watch. He told us how he felt powerless that it had happened at all and guilty that he had perceived he could have done more both during and after. This is a natural response for anyone to have, and I'm sure we've all been down that road.

At the end of yet another emotional day, our small team ventured on to the train station, hoping to be back in Manchester for later that evening. It was a solemn journey and when we weren't debriefing we were either sleeping or privately reflecting. We had ventured down to London as relative strangers yet returned very much emotionally bonded. It was a close relationship that centred on some very personal conversations and interactions. These were not colleagues or a patrol of people doing good deeds. This was a community brought together through common experience.

My own experience from having been in the military meant that bonding of this type was a common occurrence, and one that brings a certain intimacy. It's very raw work and we are of course dealing with life and death situations in the truest sense. Such interactions and circumstances really expose one human to another, and an automatic compassion develops. Love is a strong word, but there's certainly a human relationship present when such groups are brought together. I don't think any of us would ever refer to each other as best friends, but we have certainly met up since our work, and there will always be that common history that keeps us bonded by experience. I believe this happens a lot with groups such as those involved in front line and first response work.

Again, in the military, I had experience of the practice and importance of peer-to-peer support under traumatic situations. We would educate our soldiers to open up and share, and there was great encouragement to go through a self-awareness process, where members of the group share with each other everything that they did right and everything that they did wrong – or did not do at all. Such evaluation is essential for progression and closure to take place. It's hoped that such practices rid situations of stigma and shame. Heads Up CIO will always be advocates of this and have a priority to 'help the helpers' wherever we can in our work to significantly diminish any instances of secondary or vicarious trauma. Actively promoting this will be the next steps for Heads Up CIO for sure. We will help the helpers, and we will lead by example.

We alighted the train at Manchester Piccadilly both weary yet hopeful that we had perhaps done some good.

Sadly, it would be just a matter of days before Heads Up CIO would be turning their attentions to London once more.

DOV ON... PERSONAL DEVELOPMENT

I n the past year, much has changed for me. As a leader, I have become very conscious of the fact that my own learning and personal growth is ongoing and developing all the time. It's a way of leading by personal example, as the saying goes. As I learn and develop, the quality of the information I can impart to my teams becomes stronger and more relevant to them. It's about staying current and staying focused. It's a form of upgrading and reloading.

Development isn't just about getting better, stronger or faster, of course. Development is about change, resilience, and the capacity to adapt and be flexible. In my own career, I think fondly of the leaders that I served, as, whether good or bad, each of those leaders I followed taught me something, and each of those lessons was either a direct or an inadvertent opportunity to develop my own leadership style, as well as my leadership capabilities.

In my twenties, when I was in the police, I was serving as a sergeant. In that role, I oversaw 30 policemen and women. I cared for them, but I will admit that my style of leadership at the time was quite strongly autocratic. I would tell my team what to do, and I would expect it to be done. However, I quickly found that this wasn't working – either for the team, or for me, given the situations we found ourselves in. I was young, hard-headed and leading with the proverbial iron rod, and it wasn't long before my own manager called me in to see her. She began the meeting by telling me that she backed me 100%, but that she had called me in to put forward the recommendation that I think again about my style of leadership. She wanted me to consider if I honestly thought my approach was working in the best possible way in terms of getting a positive response from the team under my charge. That was all she wanted to say to me, other than an adage as I walked out of the door that, "A commander without people to command is no commander at all." In other words, my team would more than likely cease to respond to me if they even wanted to stay in the first place.

That short but positive meeting was enough to leave an impression on me. It was the start of an important journey of self-reflection and development, and it prompted me to start thinking about the long term. Ultimately, it's never about the leader, it's always about those you are aiming to lead.

Having said all this, I didn't make a change overnight. It can be hard to change everything about yourself, your behaviour and your beliefs in an instant, and there would be something disingenuous about doing so. You can't just abandon your principles or who you are. What I did do, however, was work hard and learn to adapt, and throughout all of this, my manager kept true to her word and continued to support me. In putting me first, she was practising what she preached as a leader.

LONDON'S BURNING

Whenever I think or talk about this book, I refer to it as having centred around an intensive three-week period, even though in truth the dates extended a little beyond this timescale. It was certainly intensive though, and never has the phrase *'one thing after another'* rung so true in terms of the vulnerability of society.

The 23 May was, of course, the day everything really started for me, what with it being 'the morning after the night before' of the Manchester Arena bombing in my home town of Manchester. We were now on 14 June, and I doubt I'd had a full night's sleep between those two dates. Basically, I was catching sleep whenever breaks in events, social obligation or social media would let me. I can't hide from the fact that I was always on high alert in trepidation that there might be a future event just around the corner.

Although running Heads Up CIO was extremely tiring, I gained rejuvenation in knowing that I could do some good for people. I felt fully supported always, even though I was exhausted and almost completely worn out. I was aware that people cared for me and my team and that members of the public were thankful of the support that we could give them in these worrying times.

I've talked a lot in this book about people – both friends and former strangers – who were instrumental in supporting me and everything that Heads Up CIO aimed to do in that three-week period. A key figure who I don't think I've mentioned yet was Lloyd Faber, who was a childhood friend of mine from my early life up in Glasgow. Lloyd had also gone on to serve in the military with me as a young adult. He now lived in Manchester, and his family had from an early time 'adopted' me, if you will. Since coming to Manchester myself, I had spent a lot of time with the Fabers in their family home and at family events. They were, in fact, *my* family. This was a hectic time for me, but I made sure I always had time each week to see Lloyd, his wife Rachael and his children, and I was always reminded that he was there if I needed him, even if it just meant getting out of the house to clear my thoughts or getting five minutes to myself away from everything. Seeing the devastation caused to families during the summer of 2017, I came to value my own family even more. The Fabers were a key part of that.

Whilst many of the people with me on the Heads Up CIO journey would often ask if I was okay and if they could help me, there were those who offered unofficial 'professional support' to me as well. I had met a neuro-nurse during our operations – Louise Hall – and she would be the first to remind me to sleep, before battering me into submission on the subject by reminding me about the negative psychological and physiological impacts that lack of sleep would have on me. Whenever an outside trained professional tells you that you should be doing something, you take it on board (much to the annoyance of your family and friends, who have probably been saying the same thing to you for weeks).

Sandi Mann, the clinical psychologist who had become involved in our work since we set up all things MA17, was another friend and colleague who was among the first to show and voice concern as to my wellbeing. Her main concern was that I wasn't eating. In a way, having someone question my eating habits was a bit like being a child again, but it was what I needed, and it was good that I had such caring people around me to keep me on the right path before I hit any kind of breaking point in my health or self-care.

There were, and still are, so many people who supported me personally as well as the professional objectives of Heads Up CIO during the events of that summer, and I will never be able to thank them enough. Having said that, I shall always try. I've already mentioned in this book how I felt it was my main role to help the helpers, so I guess that, in turn, it's important that I allowed people to help me.

After returning from London in the aftermath of the London Bridge and Borough Market terror attacks, our team at Heads Up CIO had little time to rest or regroup. On 14 June, reports broke in the early hours to raise the alarm of a building fire in West London's White City. My initial thought was very likely the same as everybody else's upon hearing the news – *another terror attack*. It would transpire, however, that terrorism would be ruled out quite early on in relation to this horrific event. Nevertheless, the frequency of these tragic events in the UK right now was both relentless and overwhelming.

With the cause of the fire at Grenfell Tower, a residential block, being deemed as non-terrorism related, I had to think to myself, *Can we get involved with this one?*, but the news of confirmed fatalities and the growing list of missing persons as a result of the fire was alarming. I had to have a conversation with myself. On the one hand, I needed to think about the present practical and emotional state of our team, given their intensive involvement in very recent events, but on the other hand, I needed to remember that we had set up Heads Up CIO for the prime reason of supporting people in the aftermath of trauma. It may not have been the incidence of terrorism that we had initially responded to, but it was a traumatic episode nonetheless – shock, casualties, missing persons, loss of homes, loss of life... we could make a real difference, here.

It turns out that the rest of our circle didn't really stop to question whether we would or should be involved or not, and I would face a barrage of messages that morning from our supporters, asking what our next steps would be in supporting those affected by the Grenfell Tower fire. Likewise, the posts and mentions on social media seemed to assume that Heads Up CIO would be turning its attention to the nation's capital once again.

Whilst down in London the previous week, our fantastic team had worked hard to train around 20 professional people as our next wave of volunteers in the organisation. A few of those volunteers were people who got in contact the day of the fire at Grenfell Tower. From those people, I made the move to find out if anyone was readily available to support and get themselves on site, as I was running on empty both physically and mentally, and wondered if I would logistically be able to set up anything new, so to speak. With the fire in West London still raging, I knew I would need people who were ready and willing right now.

Two people replied to me straight away to say that they could get to the scene in the first instance, but it would be wrong to use the term 'enthusiastic', because of course these offerings understandably came with questions, hesitance and worry. In theory, our volunteers were available, but in terms of what they would need to do, they had doubts.

With the fire still burning, the events at Grenfell Tower were ongoing, meaning that more and more people were becoming affected by it. It was the very definition of a traumatic event. People were still trapped, people were still unaccounted for, and more and more bodies were being identified. For everyone who had managed to escape with their lives, they will have been painfully aware that they had forever lost their homes and possessions at the very least.

Carole Galton and Yehudit Malkiel were the two volunteers from the previous training sessions in London who had responded to my request for immediate availability. I had met them briefly and remembered them from our introductions at training, but I'm sad to say that I didn't really know them at this stage. I had always thought that I would be more involved in the training we offered, but I had brought Yori over to the country to take charge of those training events and sessions. Carole and Yehudit were incredibly easy to get along with, however, and it was a privilege to work with them. They brought a lot of enthusiasm to the mammoth task ahead, and whilst that word perhaps still sounds a little inappropriate given the circumstances, we cannot underestimate how much a fresh and energetic approach is required in dealing with the mental wellbeing of those we sought to support. Around this time, I will be honest and say that I was feeling rather beaten down by everything that had happened and was continuing to happen, and so Carole and Yehudit were just the tonic I needed to refocus. On reflection, if they hadn't offered and been so proactive about the good they could do, I don't think Heads Up CIO would have got involved down at Grenfell at all.

I sometimes refer to having not been 'ready' for what we were about to deal with, but really in these circumstances, are you ever going to be? It was eating away at me thinking that whilst we had worked hard to train our volunteers down in London in terms of theory and knowledge, I wondered if we'd done enough in this time to equip them for getting out and about in the field, such as with what Carole and Yehudit were about to do now. I had no idea if the ladies even knew each other, and for some reason, it was really getting to me that they didn't even have a Heads Up CIO uniform. I needed to get them sorted with 'safety orange'.

There's a psychology around the implementation of a uniform. It's protective, emotionally as well as practically. It unifies, as the name suggests, and it provides a reassurance of togetherness, even if you don't know any of the other people dressed in it. Additionally, when you take that uniform off at the end of the day, it's a way of compartmentalising everything and distancing yourself from the event you have been party to during that time. You can change back into your own choice of clothing and begin to feel more like yourself again upon its removal. Given the work ahead of Carole and Yehudit, taking leave of their uniform at the end of the day would be as important as getting issued with one in the first place.

Some light relief was provided in our uniform task whereby the ladies showed great initiative without being dependent on me somehow getting a standard issue T-shirt to them halfway down the country. I always smile when I remember how Carole made use of her young nephew's bright orange camp T-shirt from a summer activity group he'd once been involved in. She of course turned it inside out before wearing it. It was proactive, and I liked it.

Hearing all about Carole and Yehudit's determination to get going, I faced a personal dilemma. I debated for a long time if I should jump on a train and join them, but ultimately decided that this could potentially be a waste of time and resource, given how long it would take me to get down to the site. If I'm honest with myself, I was also past the point of exhaustion. Nevertheless, I still had a role to play, and made sure that I set up all communication channels as with previous events. GT17 was born as our operational WhatsApp group, and I would monitor it from Manchester. I asked Carole and Yehudit to use the group to keep us notified of their locations and dealings, and to post photos that we could use in social media to raise awareness of our cause. All of this would really help paint a picture of events for me. As with all the WhatsApp groups, I really didn't want them to turn into chat rooms, owing to the fact that the information contained within them needed to be relevant and current. If a messaging app is constantly 'pinging', then people quickly lose both interest and focus in what is being said. Obviously, this would be counterproductive to what we wanted and needed to do.

As with every event that Heads Up CIO had been involved in, my focus was the physical safety and mental wellbeing of those under my direct or indirect leadership. This has been, and will always be, my remit as a leader. I was conscious then, that I was sending two relative strangers into a largely unknown and unpredictable situation and attempting to guide them from some 200 miles away. Remember that the blaze at Grenfell Tower was ongoing, and so both the fire and the fallout could have got much worse. This wasn't a Ground Zero situation – this was a warzone.

Before entering that warzone, I insisted that Carole and Yehudit give me the details for their next of kin in case of an emergency. In the meantime, Jo Almond, who had been so instrumental during the initial set-up of Heads Up CIO, was updating us with in-the-moment facts regarding the situation down at Grenfell Tower, including what we could expect in terms of the number of confirmed and assumed casualties. During all this communication, I reminded our volunteers to stay within legal and safe limits for anything they were wanting or needing to do, such as complying with police cordons etc. I wanted them to help, but to retreat if it became in any way apparent that their presence was a hindrance. Everything I communicated on the WhatsApp group was bullet-pointed at each stage for easy access and reference.

Based on information coming through from Jo, I told Carole and Yehudit to head to a nearby rugby club, as we'd heard via news channels that this was where people were gathering. Carole's response threw me a little. She sent a message saying, *"Dov, please can you give me background on who we actually are!"* Instantly, I was reminded of just how new this team was. In response, I directed Carole to the Heads Up CIO website that was operational at the time, and told her that what we had written on there might be a good starting point for formal and consistent introductions. Shortly after sending that message, I reminded Carole and Yehudit that they must always work together – not just in the sense of team work, but physically together for safety.

During the day, I would come to be pleasantly surprised by the efficient turn that our use of social media and messaging apps would take in aiding the efficacy of our operations. This transpired through Yehudit's decision to start using WhatsApp to record real-time voice notes, rather than having to take time out and away to 'text' through information. The voice notes would prove to be a wonderful way of documenting and receiving a running commentary of the day. In addition, I'd be able to gain extra information regarding the wellbeing of our volunteers by picking up on their tone. Yehudit, in her first message, through which she informed me that a link had been made with the Samaritans and the British Red Cross, told me that she and Carole would be moving on from the rugby club to gather at a local church, where she had been told they would be needed. She sounded calm and in control, and she sounded positive. These were all great signs both for her personal wellbeing as well as for the good of the task at hand.

As a leader, it is not lost on me that those in the field need to make decisions as they see fit. It is neither fair nor founded for somebody outside of the action to dictate the next steps if those within the field see a clear course of action and wish to take it. This is very much a military mentality, and I know that I've drawn upon that cultural way of life previously in this book. Whilst encouraging Carole and Yehudit to make decisions that they saw fit, I remained in contact and supportive, and I reminded them all along how proud I was of them.

A further update came through on WhatsApp from our team. Most people had been – or were still being – evacuated from the local area surrounding the tower block, and the good people at the church were doing all they could to support. The medics on hand were more than happy to have any professional support they could from anyone – including our team. Safe in the knowledge that they were welcome, Carole and Yehudit set about talking to people who they could see were on their own. According to their reports, they couldn't spot anyone demonstrating any signs or symptoms of shock, but they were vigilant. I felt confident from what I was hearing that all was going as well as it needed to. Our team were quickly immersing themselves in the work of other support providers and were really working as part of a multi-agency approach in making themselves practically useful to others, so their attendance was key even if they couldn't actively treat or support anyone at this stage. It was all very positive.

When people recall traumatic events that have happened to them, they cannot always distinguish between the past and the present. There will likely be holes in continuity of the recollection, so the brain will continue to go back to the event to work out what they feel is an issue with the chronology of what the person has witnessed or been involved in. This process can often result in nightmares and flashbacks, and these things can really make a person feel as though they are back involved in the event itself. Heads Up CIO train our volunteers to work through this via the adoption of a quick protocol known as memory structure intervention (MSI), which had been developed by Professor Yori Gidron. This protocol isn't therapy, debriefing or counselling, and it doesn't aim or claim to replace these things, but in the moments following a traumatic event, it can really help people to put events in order, even if some of the gaps cannot be filled. I had told Carole and Yehudit to work through MSI in conversational form with people, which they got a lot out of doing. Carole would go on to tell me that she had a conversation with a local man named Mahmood, who had witnessed people jumping from Grenfell Tower as it burned through the night. Not only is that a shocking thing to witness in the first instance, but it also carries additional trauma in the realisation that the person who jumped was doing so by choosing that option as a preferable death to the one imminent within the building itself. Mahmood was certainly in need of our intervention, and I stand by the fact that if Heads Up CIO can help even one person, then everything is, or would be, worthwhile.

Carole would soon contact me again via a voice note to ask, in her words, *"A quick question."* In her note, she documented seeing two African ladies who were clearly distressed. One of the ladies could not find her five-year-old son, having been split up from him during escape from the burning building. Naturally, she was becoming more and more hysterical because in her mind, her son must have been killed, and therefore she was already grieving. Carole's own tone revealed that she herself was distressed, so I kept vigilant regarding her wellbeing. Carole told me that she didn't think she or Heads Up CIO in general had a role in dealing with this lady. She felt that maybe things had already gone too far in terms of what the lady was going through. I viewed the fact that Carole questioning this meant that she knew this was the *exact* type of situation she was trained for, but she was clearly scared and desperately seeking guidance and reassurance from me before getting caught up in something that was already escalating. This was precisely my job – to reassure and to guide. I responded to Carole to remind her that no harm would be done by intervening, and that such intervention would not take anything away from the lady's grieving process. It was a motion that we both had to go through, and we both knew what needed to be done. Our protocols of intervention and support or treatment take just 90 seconds, and in this time, Carole's intervention would mean that the lady in question could be brought back from the acute stress reaction of psychological shock that she was going through, which could be clouding her cognitive judgement.

"How can you help me, my little boy is dead!" was the response given to Carole as she approached the grieving mother. She was in shock and fear, because the absence of a body, and the uncertainty about everything that could have possibly happened, meant that she couldn't properly grieve or rationalise about her son. At this point, the police were intervening and felt that the lady could be of real help in locating the missing boy. However, her reaction was preventing her from communicating effectively. Carole knew that her intervention could help, and after informing the police of what she was trained to do, she knelt by the mother's side and worked with her using our state-of-the-art protocol to bring her to a more responsive state. The lady became more composed due to the improved psychological state she now found herself in, and was able to speak clearly to the police to help them with their enquiries. Put simply, the lady had been moved from an overwhelming place to a place of coherence, and by working with her cognitive state, she was able to think rationally and cooperate. The police were impressed and thankful, and this was a good way of keeping good relationships and reputation with official bodies.

I wanted Carole and Yehudit to gain experience through all of this and to step outside of their comfort zones if possible, as this would help them with any future events. For Heads Up CIO to help as many people as possible, my team needed to be as experienced as possible.

Later that day, Carole would go on to actively make space for a young boy to rest amid the chaos and distress.

It will have been a good feeling for her, and a sense of real contribution. She felt effective and professional, as did Yehudit for all she had done. It was a good feeling all round that we were helping, given the circumstances.

Gathering centre at Grenfell Tower

Heads Up volunteers at Grenfell Tower

Grenfell Tower

Heads Up specialist Dr. Naomi Baum

Mission Grenfell Tower 2017

DOV ON...
EMPOWERMENT

The word 'empowerment' gets used a lot in the field of leadership – in the textbooks, in the seminars, in the motivational posts – but it can mean different things to different people. For example, some leaders will empower people under their direction by allowing them the capacity to make decisions from choices that are given to them, whilst other leaders may empower their charges by actively encouraging the decision-making capability and process to fall into their hands entirely in the first instance. The difference may be subtle, but it's there.

For me, empowerment is all about having a self-sense of being able to do something. Empowerment is an emotion, an ability and a capability to get something to happen or materialise.

As a leader, and as a believer in the culture I embraced as part of my time in the military, I believe that a responsibility of empowering is to bring these resources out in other people. For me, it's all about understanding everyone that you are working with. All human beings have general and natural ways of learning and behaving, but they also have their own unique qualities and ways of absorbing and applying what they know or learn. Every person has a unique history and value of their own, and so when we think of leadership, we should remember that although we may have responsibility for a team, that team will be made up of individuals who all require empowerment for that team to function as a whole. Leaders must look at those individuals and identify what can be taught, what can be developed and what can be enhanced. Empowerment in this way generates confidence and self-esteem, and both things are essential in allowing a leader to then work towards the next steps of the team's progression.

- A good leader will lead an individual – mentoring their development.
- A great leader will lead a team of individuals – balancing the needs of every member against the shared objectives.
- A truly exceptional leader will recognise that the team has its own dynamic, and that it is more than just a sum of its parts. A team is not a mix of personalities; it has its own personality as a unit.

Empowerment, therefore, needs to be unique to what you are presented with in your team, or with those individuals looking to you for leadership.

NOT QUITE A SIESTA

A few days, or perhaps a week, after the Grenfell Tower fire, I would find myself packing a suitcase. On this occasion, I wasn't packing in response to an urgent event or to journey down to London to show my support at a coming batch of training events. This time, I was packing my case to do something just for me.

Months before the inauguration of Heads Up CIO, and before the country descended into a spring of unease that would see a series of traumatic events unfold across two major cities, I had booked flights, accommodation and tickets for a global conference, or 'World Con', as they are often referred to by our transatlantic cousins. The conference was taking place in Seville in Spain and was officially heralded as the World Conference of the Association for Contextual Behavioural Science (ACBS). I appreciate this may alienate some readers at this point, but as I've already alluded to in this book, I'm hugely passionate about personal development, and I love to learn. Therefore, this conference had been something I'd been looking forward to attending for quite some time. During the events of the previous weeks, I'd forgotten about it, so to see an event reminder flash up on my phone was a lovely and indeed welcome surprise.

The flight across to Spain was quite surreal, in the sense that I think it was the first time in around a month that I didn't have my phone bleeping and buzzing at me with information, questions and comments. I think the captain of a plane is perhaps one of the very few people in this world who can give the instruction to turn off your phone knowing that people will take note and heed it. As I took my seat and prepared for take-off, it was nice to be alone for once (not including the 200 or so other passengers outbound to Spain).

Upon landing in Spain, I took a train to Seville. It was as soon as I got off the train at my destination that everything hit me, and even more so the next day when I got inside the venue for the conference and found out that so many people in there had been following me on social media and willing me on to do good things with Heads Up CIO. I didn't know these people, but they seemed to know me. It was truly humbling. All those people in that room had been brought together through a passion and expertise for acceptance and commitment therapy (ACT), and so in a room full of my peers, I felt incredibly valued and in a place of mutual respect. I had journeyed to this conference to see my 'celebrity' heroes, if you will, but it seemed that I had a small following all of my very own! I must admit, the positive attention, without any need to rush off and do something or make a decision, was quite a nice feeling. Being present at the conference felt to me as though I was within a cocoon of professional support. It was a truly therapeutic way to 'come down' from everything I had been going through. I felt safe.

The 'World Con' in question was a gathering of practitioners from a cohort of around 10,000 members of the ACBS. A figurehead of the group was Steven Hayes, who I have mentioned previously in this book as being a founder and a pioneer of ACT. He also happened to be somewhat of a personal hero of mine, and an unofficial mentor of sorts. His work, and the concept of ACT itself, was to be a key element of the conference that lay ahead, and the undoubted next step in my learning.

Why do I love ACT so much? It's all in the name – ACT (it's pronounced 'act' rather than three separate letters). Presumably, those in the know called it this for two reasons. One, they were tired of the acronym-ridden world of abbreviated therapy names, and two, the word implies action, and therefore has connotations of real purpose and real outcomes.

I had been delighted to read that Steven himself would be giving a workshop at the conference, because for so long I had been keen to see him in action. I hope he won't mind me saying, but he's not the youngest guy around anymore, and I wanted to see him before he decided to retire. It's much the same way that people go to watch bands in concert, in case they split up and so therefore don't get to witness their wonder anymore!

Whilst my visit to the conference came at a wonderful time for me both personally and professionally, there was also crossover in the diary that I wish could have been avoided. A colleague called Naomi Baum, whose work was known by our trustees, was due to be travelling over to Manchester that same week that I would be away, by our earlier arrangement with easyJet of flying in a team of professionals to support our cause. Naomi is a school psychologist, and was also former Director of the Resilience Unit at the Israel Center for the Treatment of Psychotrauma. In addition to this impressive CV, Naomi was also in charge of the National School Resilience Project. I'd really wanted Heads Up CIO to take direction towards working with schools and young people in future projects surrounding preparation and prevention, and so we wanted and needed Naomi's expertise in order to do this most effectively.

The initial plan had been for Naomi to come and work with Heads Up CIO for a period of a week, during which time she would deliver a series of workshops and talks in and around the North West. These were mainly in Manchester, but there were one or two reaching out as far as Liverpool. Both were key cities that could legitimately be affected by future events like the ones seen in Manchester and London in previous weeks, so their communities were ideal to work within. The locations in question included multi-faith centres and community centres, and attendees at Naomi's gatherings included a wide range of people such as the police, first responders, teachers, and even refugees who were keen to listen to any information that may help to protect them should traumatic events continue to happen. Naomi's background in giving such talks and leading her workshops was based in her work with large-scale organisations in dealing with the traumatic aftermath of terrorist attacks. I was tremendously disappointed that the timing meant that not only would I not be able to sit in on these workshops and talks, but that I wouldn't even be able to meet Naomi in person, either. Maurice and Carin would oversee taking good care of our guest in my absence, and so I was at least grateful for that.

Back to the conference, however. It was my first one, and it would also be the first time that I would be meeting my mentor, Steven Hayes, in real life. We had kept in touch via email and had chatted during a vlog I had previously put out when profiling key players within the world of ACT on my social media channels. I was very much looking forward to seeing his workshop and listening to his musings on the next phase of ACT and the development of it as a process rather than a protocol. I had always admired how Steven's thinking was that therapy in general is process-based; in other words, you go with whatever is happening to the person or client in front of you, and you don't diagnose or follow a rigid manual protocol.

My plan was to meet Steven via attendance at his workshop, and then hopefully grab some time with him later, though I knew that he would be in high demand. I was also looking forward to meeting up with some other colleagues – those I had already met elsewhere, and those whom I would be meeting for the first time having engaged in a positive dialogue with them on social media. As well as meeting all these people, however, I was looking forward to having some time to myself.

It was a good job that I wasn't banking on seeking complete solace or quiet during the trip, as from the minute I walked into the conference hall, to the moment I checked out of my hotel, the amount of people coming up to me to talk about the work I had been doing as part of Heads Up CIO was staggering. It was like I was a celebrity. It was startling, really, both in terms of the volume of attention and in terms of the recognition for everything that Heads Up CIO had set out to do. It was inspiring in the sense that I felt compelled to carry on our good work and to harness the power of social media and networking to promote positive messages and effects. To keep doing good work, we'd need recognition and backing, and places like this conference could prove to be an excellent starting point.

During the conference, I felt very much at home, surrounded by a cohort of my peers. I love everything about ACT, and this was the perfect place to develop both personally with fellow attendees and professionally through partaking in events run by my heroes and mentors, even though to this day I will never refer to myself as a fellow academic. One of the people I had signed up to see in a workshop was Louise Hayes – no relation to Steven – who is from Australia. Her area of expertise lay in dealing with adolescence. I had told Louise that I wanted to work in schools and predominantly with teenagers, and she was up for supporting me in terms of resource as well as knowledge.

It was incredibly strange hearing my name called to me so often at the event. Sure, there were faces I recognised and names that were familiar upon introduction, but I felt uncomfortable that I didn't know a lot of these people. It was the start of a true journey of self-reflection, and after a wonderful week in Spain, I packed my bags to return home.

As the plane ascended on take-off, it struck me that I was still very much personally on a comedown. The adrenaline, the reactivity, the trepidation… it had all been a lot to take. Whilst I had been grateful for the week away, I needed to crystallise everything that I thought and wanted to happen once I would get back home. I'd thought for so long about what we were doing, but now I could think reflectively about all that we had already done. That week had transported me to a whole new place, both literally and metaphorically. I really hadn't thought I'd have been so 'up' for socialising, but not only did I enjoy it, I realised how much I needed it. It was a form of therapy for me, you could say. What I could not – and still can't – understand, is how much of an impact the work of Heads Up CIO was having across the world, it seemed. I had always wanted our work to benefit human life and believed that if just one human being could be affected positively, then our work was doing nothing but good things.

After a few days, I had realised exactly what I wanted to do, both personally and with Heads Up CIO. I was now more connected, better resourced, and – to some extent – refreshed having been removed, albeit temporarily, from everything that had been going on.

During that plane journey home, I honestly couldn't tell you what was going through my head, and in part, the one or three whiskies I'd had from the bar played a small role in that. I felt good, and it felt even better not having to communicate with anyone, if just for a few hours. I would later post on social media that my week away had involved learning, experiencing, socialising, resting, crying, laughing, reflecting, and many other mindful moments.

When I got home, there was a letter waiting for me. In fact, there was a pile of mail, as is usually the case after having been away, but one letter stood out. It was from Kensington Palace. After the attack on the arena and our consequent work in Manchester, you will remember the invitation bestowed upon Heads Up CIO to meet HRH Prince William, Duke of Cambridge, along with a group of other first responders, whose roles had been so instrumental in the city in the aftermath of the arena bombing. You may also remember that my colleague Susan had given HRH Prince William one of our 'safety orange' Heads Up CIO T-shirts as a gift, just prior to us cheekily hinting that he might consider being a patron of our charity. At the time, the Prince had thanked me politely before his secretary took the shirt from him for safe-keeping, whilst William carried out the rest of his duties. The letter I was holding in my hands right now was one thanking me for the gift of the T-shirt and offering yet more praise for the work that Heads Up CIO had done for the people of Manchester following the terrible events of that night in late May. It was lovely to receive the letter, but it was even better to know that Prince William had personally taken receipt of the gift. I'm under no illusions to think that His Royal Highness is, or was, wearing the T-shirt when not out on royal tours of duty, but it was good to know that it was at least being cared for and appreciated by its intended recipient.

At the time, the royal meeting had been a wonderful experience, but I had never quite realised the impact. Even without the Prince as our patron (though he is still yet to say no), the coverage gave us the recognition we needed to grow, and for our work to be taken seriously on an established scale among our peers.

Over the next few days, I gave myself somewhat of a break. I should have stayed a little longer in Seville, and though I'd had a few days of free time there, I was eager to continue with some much-needed rest and relaxation back home. Whilst everyone deserves a holiday and to take some time for themselves without any need to explain or justify this to anyone, I knew some me-time was going to be essential if I was going to go full throttle at the next stage of development for Heads Up CIO. How can you care for others if you cannot care for yourself?

On 5 July, feeling reflective and refreshed, I took to social media, and began work. My starting point would be a message of recognition and thanks for all that Heads Up CIO had achieved so far. It read as follows:

Heads Up CIO would like to begin by thanking all of our volunteers. It is only with your commitment to training and compassionate gifting of your time that, together, we have been able to provide CORTEX-cognitive psychological first aid to those affected by recent terrorist attacks and tragic events.
- *With your help, and the help of many generous people and businesses, we have achieved:*
- *The training of 68 mental health therapists, counsellors and psychologists in cognitive psychological first aid*
- *The set-up of three pop-up treatment centres in London and Manchester*
- *Active response to three major traumatic events – Manchester Arena, London Bridge and Grenfell Tower*

- *Provision of direct support for over 100 people affected by terrorism and major incidents*
- *Receipt of initial and CPD training from three international specialists*
- *Exposure from over 30 press, TV and radio interviews across three countries and continents*
- *A royal audience from HRH Duke of Cambridge (Prince William)*
- *Putting Heads Up CIO on the emergency services map!*

PRETTY GOOD GOING IN THE SPACE OF JUST ONE MONTH!

Thank you all so much! Onward – we have much work to do.

Whilst a qualitative and emotive approach is always likely to be warmly welcomed by those who play a part in such a positive mission, having quantitative data to hand to support our successes and document our achievements was a fantastic thing to share, even though we had additionally helped hundreds of others directly and indirectly through our work in the streets of Manchester and London. It would also no doubt be a great basis from which to showcase proven results and impact, should we find ourselves in a place whereby we could apply for funding to support and enhance our future work.

At the beginning of this journey, I didn't want any money, and I remembered how adamant and even annoyed I was when I approached people for support and they just assumed I was after cash (when I really wasn't). I just wanted action. Coming back from Spain, however, I realised that if we were ever going to do anything bigger and better for the good of the public in helping them 'the day before' – preventative work, rather than just on the day or in the aftermath of a traumatic event – then we would indeed need money. Wonderful as it had been, the generosity already bestowed on us wasn't going to last forever.

I needed to start thinking about fundraising, and I needed to take seriously what is an enormous task for any organisation looking to acquire a considerable amount of funds and resources to carry out their work. I was to find out quite quickly that fundraising is anything but fun, and rather, it's a warzone of networking, admin and bureaucracy. It's finding funding, filtering facts and filling in forms. It's no longer what I was used to in my role, which had been all about strategy, action and adrenaline, but I knew that as soon as I got funding into place, I could get myself back out there into the field to start helping people.

I have to admit that, the more I thought about it, the less I did. I didn't know where to start.

As it turned out, however, a great opportunity would present itself in the form of the 'We Love Manchester' fund, which was set up in the aftermath of the Manchester Arena bombing. This seemed like a 'dead cert' of a place to start, and so once applications were open, we submitted a case for our charity. The good people behind the fund initially accepted our application and kept in close contact with us – asking questions, seeking data and clarifying research. They certainly made us do our homework, that's for sure. Eventually though, the answer was 'No'. It was a very short email of response, which simply stated that they would not fund something that a statutory service should be doing. In our case, they claimed that the NHS could provide what we were offering. I immediately contested the decision on those grounds, because surely our point was that although other services *should* be providing our offer, they simply were not…? It didn't matter, however, and the people at the fund showed, after many emails, that they were now no longer interested in funding our vital work to fill a gap in the provision of CORTEX-CPFA and the treatment of trauma in the aftermath of an event. I tried one last time with a plea stating that not only was our work unique in terms of provision, but that it was unique on a national scale. It didn't matter – no meant no.

We would go on to be unsuccessful with our second attempt at a funding application, also. This time, the submission was to an organisation called Big Potential Advanced. We only found out about this opportunity with six hours to spare, so I must be honest and say that the application probably wasn't the best piece of admin I've ever prepared. Although the application was marked as unsuccessful, I have to say that I was delighted with the correspondence from the funding body. Firstly, they took the time to tell us about how they believed our project was 'interesting and innovative'. Secondly, and most importantly, they took the time to detail the sections of our application that fell short in terms of meeting requirements. They had essentially 'marked' our application, meaning that, should we write one again, we'd know all the pitfalls to avoid and all the areas in which we'd need to tighten up or expand. It was hugely advantageous.

Our third attempt was to apply for funding under the National Lottery 'Awards For All' application scheme. It wouldn't need to be third time lucky, it would need to be third time 'right'.

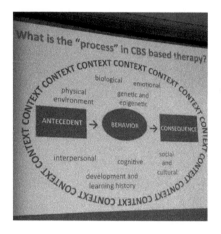

CBS workshop at Worldlon, Seville

In Seville with Steven Hayes

Testimonial: Anna Watkinson.
This is a marvellous act of kindness and needed after such a shocking and tragic week. It's so important that people talk and discuss their feelings to like-minded and understanding people. I am from Manchester or to be exact, Salford, and have been living in Australia for over 10yrs. I watched the news everyday last week and was so so upset, angry and so proud of everyone. I've cried every day and grieved for the people and the city. I've felt so alone as nobody here has mentioned it to me. I've not been able to let my feelings out and I've felt so helpless being so far away. I am coming over in 6 weeks time and can't wait to hug my friends and sit and pray in St Anne's church, buy merchandise and donate to the charities. I hope I can talk to my fellow Mancunians and help myself as well as others come to terms with this terrible event. It just in some ways reminded me of the IRA days and again bad memories came flooding back. So as I say well done to everybody concerned in opening this drop-in centre to help people with the tragic event of Mon 22nd May and I look forward to seeing my friends and Manchester in July.

Support for MA17 Support Centre

DOV ON... 'NOT' BEING AN ACADEMIC

A good read of this book and a glance at my profile as I continue with my work with Heads Up CIO may paint a picture of me that I do not believe is entirely accurate. That picture may be one of me as an academic. I'm not.

Looking back over my life, I have had somewhat of a history of obtaining scholarly placements despite not being a typical applicant. For example, I got accepted into a prestigious law school despite not even finishing high school back in Glasgow. I think by the time I'd decided I wanted to work towards a law degree to follow a passion of mine, I was able to present the university admissions team with little more than the equivalent of half an 'A' Level. With determination, however, I ended up studying for an LLB in Law and a BA in Government and specialising in terrorism concurrently; such was my commitment to following my interests. Whilst it's always important to follow your interests, I think it's even more important to send a message out that it's never too late to learn, and that you can always draw on other qualities to get you on that pathway. As a youngster, I had never been the most academic of students, and I believed I struggled more than my peers at times, but this never stopped my self-belief in wanting to try and not being afraid to 'fail', even though I still struggle with things now and always doubt my true capabilities. As it would turn out, this level and topic of study would prove to come in very useful later in life as I set up Heads Up CIO.

Whilst I'm sure that many academics would view it differently, in my opinion, being an academic is a state of mind. If we talk about it as being someone who holds multiple degrees and a track record of study throughout their industry and career, then that's not what I want to be recognised for. My focus is on gaining new knowledge and being a part of things when that knowledge has the chance to develop or evolve. I enjoy research and I love being involved in it. When I get to see what I've learned be put into practice and indeed have an impact, it's a complete joy to me. It's productive and it's creative.

I think my passion for creativity within study is why I'm such a big supporter of acceptance and commitment therapy (ACT). I admire how Steven Hayes works and what he does to engage people in his revolutionary approaches to psychological treatments. It comes down to even the smallest of things, whereby he will even create new yet simple mid-terms in which to explain things to therapists and clients alike, such as the term 'defuse' – a word for the process of becoming less rigid or unmoving in your approach. To defuse is to unhook from certain mindsets and to become more open. I love the word, and I love the concept, too.

Though my academic focus and backing for what I put together for Heads Up CIO has always centred on CORTEX-CPFA and the work of my unofficial mentor, Dr Farchi, ACT is something that our organisation will always look to adopt as a progressive way of truly treating people, including ourselves for self-care and resilience, who can benefit from it as a process. It's an integral part of working with our people. As the acronym even suggests, ACT is about action. And so are we!

For me, true academia is a combination of commitment to traditional ways of working, with an open outlook to future developments. In the case of ACT, involvement within it doesn't require me – or indeed anyone who practises it – to be an academic. In fact, I think it's the only mainstream therapy that holds no hierarchical barrier to entry. There is no formal examination to take or subscription to pay, and there is no accreditation that you can show to the world to say that you are a master practitioner. I think the 'open source' idea that Steven Hayes had behind ACT, was that if it was being used at all, in any creative way, then it was doing some good. Applying any kind of knowledge should always be about creating something positive – not about having another certificate to hang on your wall.

THE WHAT
AND THE HOW

Heads Up CIO was born to fill a gap and to take bold action.

- The gap: a dedicated emergency response to casualties of psychological injury immediately following terrorist and mass casualty events.
- Bold action: creating a national programme that will reach out with speed, compassion and professionalism in the service of preventing and treating costly psychological and behavioural problems due to stress and trauma caused by terrorist action and mass casualty events.

Our aim:

1. To educate, prepare and train the general population for future mass casualty disasters to reduce risk of trauma and further complications, build capacity to deal with major events, improve resilience and mental health whilst simultaneously lowering risk for anxiety, stress and depression.

2. To provide CORTEX-cognitive psychological first aid (CPFA) and resilience training to mental health professionals, first-responders, emergency staff and the public.

3. To provide a free-at-point-of-service emergency response service for the psychologically injured at mass casualty events due to terrorist action, natural and man-made hazards, criminal behaviour or accidents. Caring for those affected while the other emergency services get on with the job.

4. To develop and build strong, resilient, caring and nurturing individuals within the different communities of the UK (and further afield) by encouraging and training more people to be proactive in responding and working together.

How is this done?

1. Providing a voluntary-based free-at-point-of-service emergency response team to reach the scene of traumatic events with speed, compassion and professionalism. (This will reduce the need to evacuate to expensive A&E units and improve the efficiency of the mass casualties disaster management by allowing self-evacuation and lowering risks of mass hysteria, community trauma and chaos.)

2. Providing a site-specific, follow-up clinic immediately following such events to provide professional support to reduce the psychological impact of trauma.

3. Providing a national standard prevention training programme to create a state of preparedness for the

general population, professional and emergency staff in how to cope with the stress and trauma following terrorism and other mass casualty events.

Whilst I've wanted this book to serve as a narrative surrounding the tragic events of spring 2017 and how Heads Up CIO came into fruition in order to help survivors of each of those traumatic events, I think it would be a wasted opportunity if I didn't at some point in the documentation reveal a little about the training that our organisation has delivered to our wonderful teams – the same CORTEX-CPFA training we wish to offer to as many people as possible as we build our charity into the future as providers of standardised intervention.

In an ideal world, I believe that you can only ever really gain so much from reading about any kind of training, and that you should always try to engage or get involved in a training event, such as ours, in person if you get the opportunity.

The rise of traumatic events amongst many populations has led to greater exposure to traumatic events worldwide, including terror attacks, conflicts, interpersonal violence, severe car accidents and natural disasters. Internationally, the impact of trauma-related disorders is becoming increasingly concerning. Research and experience indicate that for every patient who is physically injured, there are a further 15–25 people who are psychologically injured.

The five most commonly reported traumatic events, accounting for over half of all exposures, include witnessing death or serious injury, the unexpected death of a loved one, being mugged, being in a life-threatening automobile accident and experiencing a life-threatening illness or injury.

The evidence is clear: immediate support is essential to stem the flow of mental health issues and mental illness resulting from these horrific events. Complications such as post-traumatic stress disorder (PTSD) are expected to affect many of the population directly as well as having an impact on services and wider society.

The current generalised approach to early intervention in the immediate aftermath of a traumatic event is psychological first aid (PFA). PFA is built on the concept of resilience, designed to help people in the immediate aftermath of any emergency and based on an understanding that people affected by traumatic events will experience early stress reactions which may cause sufficient distress to impede adaptive coping, and recovery. Therefore, PFA is intended to reduce the initial acute stress reaction (ASR) caused by events which are perceived as traumatic, and to foster short- and long-term adaptive functioning and coping. PFA is currently recommended by the World Health Organization (WHO) as an alternative to debriefing and it is being implemented nowadays by the British Red Cross. It has been broadly endorsed by disaster mental health experts, in the peer-reviewed disaster behavioural health literature and is also consistently recommended in international treatment guidelines.

However useful and providing a framework to intervene during the immediate hours or days after a traumatic event, PFA guidelines suffer from several limitations: they focus on the 'what to do' and 'what not to do' but fall short of explaining exactly 'how to do it'. In addition, they are basically designed to provide help in a context in which an emergency response system is in place and are not specifically designed to be used in the immediate minutes following an emergency event, but hours or even days after the event has occurred and once a disaster response system is in place.

To fill in the gap of the above-mentioned limitations, Heads Up CIO provides a new form of PFA – CORTEX-CPFA. CORTEX-CPFA has two main components: first, it is designed in the framework of the WHO guidelines for PFA but, second, it includes a new PFA approach, the Six Cs model – immediate cognitive-functional psychological first aid (ICF-PFA). This model provides a standardised intervention during an ASR to shift the person from a helpless, passive and incompetent state into a state of active efficient functioning, within several minutes after the traumatic event. The model is based on four theoretical and empirically tested concepts: (1) hardiness, (2) sense of coherence, (3) self-efficacy, and (4) the neuropsychology of the stress response, focusing on shifting people from a limbic system hyperactivity to a pre-frontal cortex activation during stressful events. This model by no means endorses any form of 'debriefing' or psychological ventilation which is contrary to the model's neuropsychological basis. On the contrary, and based on evidence-based human and animal studies regarding the stress response, the model intends to promote activation of the cognitive thinking part of the brain – the CEO (pre-frontal cortex) – through cognitive-focused interventions that help reduce the stress response and down-regulate the emotional part of the brain (the amygdala). In addition, the model's aim is to shift the processing of traumatic memories from a fragmented and emotional (limbic) dominance mode to a more organised and cognitive-thinking mode (pre-frontal processing) – a shift from narrative-based and emotion-focused interventions into cognitive-focused interventions.

There are two parts to our Heads Up CIO training in CORTEX-CPFA. Part one is a theoretical introduction to the process, and part two is an opportunity for practical application of what the training hopes to achieve in bringing survivors to a state of cognition for them to function effectively in the aftermath of psychological shock. Essentially, we are looking at how to bring a person from helplessness and passiveness into active and effective function.

Part one welcomes all of our volunteers together, and to maximise our session together we get straight to work in exploring the defence systems of the brain and how they work. The foundations of this element are based in neuroscience, but we work hard to make sure that our training is engaging and that our information is put forward clearly, concisely and in accessible terms. You don't have to be from a scientific background to learn or apply our training, but whilst there's no getting away from the psychological and pathological significance behind our work, it's important that anyone can and should get involved in it.

To start, the session allows time to explore the theory behind the brain's pre-frontal cortex, located just behind the eyes. This is the part of the brain that distinguishes us from other creatures as being human. I like to refer to it as the CEO of the brain, as it controls and is responsible for many things, such as problem-solving, logic, calculation and management of emotions. These can be described as executive functions of the brain, and those that allow us to navigate and cope with everyday life. It's all about thinking and managing.

We dig a little further during our training to explore other parts of the brain, so that the significance of the pre-frontal cortex can really be appreciated. We look at and talk about the reptilian brain, which is the 'basic' brain, although given its responsibility for sustaining life systems including respiration, reproduction and digestion, it seems wrong to refer to it as anywhere close to basic. We share this reptilian brain with many creatures, and, in addition to its life systems, it's also the part of the brain that operates our responses of fight, flight or freeze in the face of perceived or real danger.

Perhaps one of the most important parts of the brain that we talk about during our training, however, is the mammalian brain, also known as the limbic system. This is the emotional part of the brain, and within it we find the amygdala, which is very much like an alarm-scanning system. It looks out for danger and has the capacity to sense it at any time it may possibly strike. During any moments of perceived or real danger, the amygdala doesn't allow us to make any kind of informed or conscious choice about what to do in response. Instead, it takes the choice right out of our hands and connects with the reptilian brain to result in our automatic response, and that response will be linked to fight (getting ready to engage in action), flight (getting ready to run away), or freeze (being unable to physically do anything at all).

Once we've talked through all of this, the training focuses back on the pre-frontal cortex and the important role it plays in fight, flight or freeze situations. Put simply, the pre-frontal cortex cannot function at the same time as the amygdala, but it can be brought back 'online' in a human being, to assess if the danger is still present or real at all. If it does not believe there is danger, it turns off the 'alarm' from the amygdala and allows the person to cognitively function once more.

The amygdala is a key element of the emotional part of the brain and can be triggered by as much as a sense or association with fear. So, for example, if you've had a bad experience with a dog at a prior point in your life – perhaps one chased, bit or generally just scared you – then if you hear a dog bark, even though it's nowhere near you, the amygdala can trigger that alarm of evoking a response to what it assumes is a threat. In some people, the amygdala can be quite hyperactive, and this can result in alarms being set off in the absence of even a direct association. For example, say you were bitten by a dog in a park with swings, then being near a park with swings, with no hint of a canine anywhere in earshot or eyeline, can be enough of an association to set the amygdala into action. This can all become even further removed from direct association, with the person even being sent into panic if they happen to be in the same city as where the fearful event took place. It's known as hypervigilance, and it sparks avoidance in the person it affects.

In an extreme traumatic event such as being present in a location where a bomb goes off, as with the Manchester Arena terror attack, whether real or perceived, the response is the fear that you're going to die or be significantly injured. The pre-frontal cortex (your sense of control) and your amygdala (your panic alarm) simply cannot function at the same time, and so the amygdala will effectively shut down the pre-frontal cortex. The result is that you may go into psychological shock. You may subsequently struggle with any kind of rationalisation, including problem-solving, co-ordination, knowing where you are, grasping time, emotional regulation and spatial awareness. You may be disoriented to say the least. In addition, all these things will make you feel incredibly alone, and you will not be able to see or feel a connection to anyone. It's a truly frightening scenario.

When the amygdala is in charge, the fight, flight or freeze system is 'online'. Fight means that you accept the danger or threat and you will attempt to tackle it. Flight means you'll seek to get away or out of the situation. Freeze means exactly that – you'll be physically unable to do anything, as both your body and your brain shut down the ability to move or perhaps even speak. In these cases, the body can go into what's known as a catatonic state.

There have often been arguments regarding the relationship between the brain and the body when it comes to what is the higher power to a person's response to psychological shock. I tell those I work with that the brain can be considered as a greedy organ, and that it will take everything it needs before distributing anything to the rest of the body. It processes what it needs, and what it doesn't. For example, if it's dealing with shock, or anxiety, then one of the last things the brain needs to do is to process digesting that sandwich you had an hour ago. It may seem simplistic, but that's why you'll feel (and often hear) things in your stomach when you are feeling nervous, anxious or excited, and why the last thing you ever want to do in those situations is to eat anything. The digestion process is somewhat halted or shut down, and this can cause issues for your body in the long term if prolonged, but you are safe in the knowledge that your brain is doing everything it needs to do in the short term to keep you safe and alive.

What has psychological first aid been until now? What did we have prior to the cognitive approach put forward by Heads Up CIO? We had the advice and protocols of the World Health Organization and the British Red Cross, which are both fantastic organisations, but ones that have championed the model of support that lies in meeting the physical needs of the victim – food, water, safety etc. It also champions the process of providing comfort and emotional support, but as we've already alluded to, adding emotion is not necessarily advantageous in these acute emergency situations. Consider this: have you ever been in an emotional state, for whatever reason, and somebody gives you a hug and says, "Are you okay?" What's the first thing you do? I am taking more than an educated guess here when I say that I'd put money on your response being one of tears. The emotional brain doesn't need more emotion to fuel its fire – it needs cognition at this critical time.

So, zoning in on the part of our training that I'm sure you're all keen to read about so that you can go out and sign up for your nearest course... what does our Heads Up CIO protocol for applying CORTEX-CPFA consist of? In simple terms, it's the Six Cs, first pioneered by our friend, Dr Farchi.

The first C is all about **COGNITION** and remembering that the aim of the training is to work with someone to bring them back to a state of cognition, and to trigger their pre-frontal cortex so that it brings it back 'online' and overrides the amygdala. How do we do this? We look at the other five Cs...

COMMUNICATION – Talk to the person and encourage them to talk back to you in return, if possible. Ask them questions that allow them to recall information, such as their name, date of birth, where they live, etc. You can squeeze the person's hand and ask them to do the same to you, so that you can establish that communication is happening effectively, all the while explaining what you are doing, as this also serves as effective communication. In the case of a person either being physically unable to speak, or if they speak a different language to you, you can improvise with gesturing and body language. There is always a way for communication to be made.

CHALLENGE – It's important to challenge the brain function of the person you are dealing with, so following on from the communication you have established, you can progress to giving them choices, such as asking the person what they'd like to do, or giving them options to act upon, such as taking a walk with you, or going to sit in a different place. The aim is to allow the person you are dealing with the opportunity to begin to utilise their brain to recall, process and apply cognition through action. Remember that the brain must begin to problem solve for the pre-frontal cortex to come back online, so even presenting them with some simple maths questions can help.

COMMITMENT – In situations where the pre-frontal cortex has gone 'offline' because of having been replaced by the actions of the amygdala, it's extremely hard for the person involved to connect or to feel connection with anybody, so as a result, they will feel lonely and perhaps even completely alone. Letting them know that you are there with them and openly telling them that you are going to stay with them will have an incredibly positive effect in helping them make the switch in getting their pre-frontal cortex to kick back in.

CONTROL – A sense of agency or empowerment is vital in enabling a person who is suffering from psychological shock or trauma to get back to a state of cognition. It's always intuitive in these situations to do things for the person in question to help them, because we think we are doing a positive thing by taking pressure away from them. In fact, the opposite is what we should be doing, as it's vital to give that person an element of control. So, instead of getting them a glass of water or a blanket, for example, ask them to go and get one for themselves. Even a small task or action that they need to carry out is a big achievement in these cases. Getting that person to do something for someone else is even better, so asking them to count people or to help you by getting out their mobile phone and dialling a number are fantastic sample tasks.

This also serves a dual purpose, as you will be able to see the cognition when they recognise their phone and show they know what to do with it.

CONTINUITY – A function of the cognitive memory is to recall things in chronological order. However, a person suffering from psychological shock may be confused and their brain may register and recall events differently. After a few hours, that memory becomes solidified, and the brain may struggle to make sense of the order, so as a result, it will keep revisiting the memory to make things make sense. This is part of what's happening when people suffer from flashbacks and nightmares, and it can cause real problems within a person's mental health if it goes on for a significant period. The whole concept of continuity as our final 'C' is to provide the person affected with one past, one present and one future piece of relative information, so that they can at least begin to piece things together around a structure that they have experienced. The focus is to help with chronology, so something simple like, "There was an explosion earlier on, you're talking with me right now, and we're going to go sit down and have drink," is a solid start. Anything that can put a structure in place will help. It's a very powerful trigger for the immediate cognition of the affected person and is certainly a large factor in lowering the risk of long-term ASD and PTSD. It highlights that the traumatic event has ended and that the immediate threat is over.

All these Cs can be carried out in just 120 seconds. The first time you try them, you may not be able to do all of them, and you may even forget one or two, but each technique applied will be of huge significance and help when supporting a person going through psychological shock to get back to a cognitive state, whereby their pre-frontal cortex is neurologically triggered, and they can start functioning once more. An easy way of remembering what to do with the Six Cs is by using the acronym CORTEX.

- Connection – Mirror the person affected's position and establish communication.
- Obligation – Engage and commit to the person affected.
- Regain control – Engage the person affected in actions to regain control through simple tasks.
- Task – Reactivate the victim with simple tasks.
- Establish chronology – Reframe the event: past–present–future.
- EXchange – Transfer responsibilities by recruiting the person affected to actively help and assist.

It's important to note that our training does not encourage any kind of psychological ventilation and does not provide a process of psychological or stress debriefing.

Part two of our training at Heads Up CIO is split into two sections. Firstly, our participants pair up and practise applying the language of the processes they have learned. This allows them to get into a rhythm for what they need to say and do as part of their newly acquired protocols. Only when our participants have done this several times to begin embedding the 'script' do we progress to the second section, which sees our participants progressing to involvement in planned scenarios with trained actors and actresses, so that any enactments can be as intensive and realistic as possible, whereby the participant isn't simply 'going through the motions' with somebody they've just sat in a classroom with. The reason that we don't go straight into this second part is because it is too intense, and the participant subconsciously mirrors the emotions and distresses of the person they are trying to help, which, as you can imagine, isn't going to be helpful or useful in intervening. This is understandable when you think about the fact that applying CORTEX-CPFA is counter-intuitive, when natural instincts would push you to either share the panic or perhaps become too empathetic and add emotions into the mix. Emotion needs to be replaced by logical thought, and therefore we need to distance emotion from the situation for this to happen at this time.

As with doctors, all therapists and practitioners have a duty. In medicine it's the Hippocratic Oath, and in therapy it's the code of what is known as 'bioethics'. Both approaches follow the principles that the practitioner must not only seek to do good but must also do no harm. In the case of our training, I believe that if you are in receipt of the knowledge and application to carry out CORTEX-CPFA, you must do so. Not only will your intervention help somebody in the short term, but its effect could have a significant impact on their long-term mental health and wellbeing, also. You may not think it, and you may never even know it, but your actions in applying the principles of CORTEX-CPFA could save someone's life.

I'm a believer in the fact that taking part in our training – or any training for that matter – allows you to put ideas into practice, carry out application of techniques in controlled yet realistic scenarios, and of course ask any questions about everything we are seeking to achieve. But, if simply skimming through this chapter has done enough to give you the motivation to learn more of the techniques you could apply in helping a person to reach a cognitive state after suffering or witnessing psychological shock, then this is fantastic news.

CORTEX-cognitive psychological first aid. It's accessible, it's applicable and the results are achievable. This chapter is not intended as a substitute for full training. I hope we can prove this to you at a training session near you soon.

Davidson, S. (2010) The development of the British Red Cross' psychosocial framework: CALMER. *Journal of Social Work Practice*, 24, 29–42.

Farchi, M. et al. (2018) The SIX Cs model for immediate cognitive psychological first aid: from helplessness into active efficient coping. (In preparation)

Rothbaum, B. O. et al. (2012) Early intervention may prevent the development of posttraumatic stress disorder: a randomized pilot civilian study with modified prolonged exposure. *Biol. Psychiatry*, 72(11), 957–963.

Shapiro, E. (2012) EMDR and early psychological intervention following trauma. *European Review of Applied Psychology*, 62(4), 241–251.

Soldatos, C. R., Paparrigopoulos, T. J., Pappa, D. A. & Christodoulou, G. N. (2006) Early post-traumatic stress disorder in relation to acute stress reaction: an ICD-10 study among help seekers following an earthquake. *Psychiatry Res*, 143(2-3), 245–253.

World Health Organization (2015) *The ICD-10 Classification of Mental and Behavioural Disorders*. Version: 2015.

World Health Organization, War Trauma Foundation & World Vision International (2011) *Psychological first aid: Guide for field workers – World Health Organization*.

Zohar, J. et al. (2009) Can posttraumatic stress disorder be prevented? *CNS Spectr.*, 14(1 Suppl 1), 44–51.

DOV ON...
MENTAL FITNESS

always speak with colleagues and friends alike about how mental health isn't particularly based on fact; it is subjective. You can't do a blood test, X-ray or any kind of ultrasound to see or understand what's going on in somebody's mind. This is further compacted when we consider the fact that there are two main published manuals regarding mental health disorders: the American version (*Diagnostic and Statistical Manual of Mental Disorders*) versus the European version (*International Classification of Disease*). Both manuals are different in terms of what they classify as a mental health disorder. It sounds harsh, but it's kind of an autocratic system whereby the board for each of the two entities decides by process of a vote what 'classifies' as a disorder. This vote is carried out only every few years. Every time that vote takes place, a new edition of the book is published. The American version is presently on the 5th edition, whilst the European version is on its 11th. Each time this book is published, it gets bigger, as society accepts more and more separate definitions as different disorders. These disorders become medicalised and subsequently treated with medicines or therapies. In the case of medicines, these tend to treat the symptoms rather than the cause, and therefore although I am not against pharmacotherapy, I am a big advocate for evidence-based experiential psychotherapies, techniques and interventions – just like the ones we offer at Heads Up CIO.

Mental fitness needs to start with prevention. As a society we need to nurture good mental hygiene and useful behaviour from as young as possible. This is achieved by education and practice – educating our young people about how our brain works, including its generation of thoughts, sensations and emotions and their (sometimes very uncomfortable) manifestation in our bodies. This is a normal healthy process that today we pathologise and medicalise. Our perpetual chase after happiness without allowing ourselves to be sad is an example of shutting off a large part of our emotional portfolio and in the long term this will prove to be detrimental to our wellbeing. So, too, our behaviour. If we are passive and reactionary in our behaviour, eventually it manifests itself in more 'automatic behaviour'. We lose the skill to make choices and eventually we may live our lives, but if we don't participate in our lives, it becomes one big habit. We become slaves to our habits. Instead we need to nurture a more active, mindful life by learning and practising using our five senses to pay more attention to what we experience in our outer environment and to use our minds to pay attention and observe our thoughts, emotions and physical sensations within our bodies, for what they are, without judging if they are good or bad. By doing this, we can build an intimate relationship with ourselves – get to know and observe ourselves. With some self-compassion we can learn to accept ourselves for who we are – unique individuals with unique histories and experiences of unique value; I am who I am. We are not broken, and we don't need fixing.

By discovering who and what is important to us, in what valued way we want to live our lives in all our different domains – as an individual, as a brother or sister, as a parent, as a friend, as an employee, as an employer and the list of domains go on – we can create for ourselves a unique compass showing us our own valued direction in which we wish to lead our lives. Once we discover these values we can pursue them with passion and motivation regardless of the uncomfortable thoughts, feelings and sensations that we may experience from time to time. I like to use the example of the Olympic athlete whose value is achievement, acknowledged by a possible gold medal, four years away! And yet the athlete will pursue their valued life by practising their sport in all weathers and conditions, getting up early and enduring physical and emotional pain. How is it that they can endure such conditions? Their thoughts constantly telling them that *I am not good enough*. Maybe these thoughts are telling them that *I am wasting my time* and with that they experience changing emotions and uncomfortable physical sensations of anxiety and yet they persevere. I believe it's their sense of value put together with active mindful behaviour that creates the motivation for going forward. We too can implement this in our everyday lives. Identifying our values and applying the appropriate behaviour can bring vitality and motivation to our lives and create an environment of mental fitness.

Disseminating these processes, throughout our families and communities, of being more aware of ourselves, accepting of ourselves without judgement, together with our value compass, will empower us to move towards a lifestyle of mental fitness with resilience and strong inner resources. Nurturing a more psychologically flexible self better prepares us for the day-to-day bumps that life presents. Through this we can develop over time, and through practice, a healthier mind and body, reduce unnecessary suffering (mental and physical) and build a society based on wellbeing through adaptive useful and healthy behaviours.

ARE YOU READY?

As you reach the end of this book, you'll be familiar with the fact that I've interspersed it with articles and views that I used during 2017 in social media posts and during events that I've been fortunate to attend, lead and present at as part of my role in promoting and sharing the good work of Heads Up CIO. This final chapter is perhaps an extended version of something that I would 'put out there' in terms of sharing my views – and those of the charity – with the wider world. The concept in general surrounds the notions of preparedness and preventative measures.

All my work, as documented in this book, has centred on what the Heads Up CIO charity has needed to do in order to react to the terrible events that affected the UK in the spring of 2017, prior to this book being published. The book has examined, to some extent, the day *of* each of the tragic events. To an even larger degree, the book has examined the day *after* in each case. However, for me, and for Heads Up CIO, the main focus should always be on the day *before*…

I know that concept may sound ridiculous, because we can't possibly predict when any kind of event may happen in the future, or what impact they will leave in their wake. What we *can* do, however, is to anticipate what might one day happen, and we can certainly also learn from history. The more recent, the better.

As individuals and as a society, we cocoon ourselves in a feeling of 'it won't happen to me' and thus dismiss the concept of any negative possibility occurring in our lives. Some of us take a different view, however, in the desperate hope that something will never happen to us at all, and thus actively avoid certain situations altogether. An example of this is flying on an aeroplane... you can't possibly be involved in an air disaster if you never board a plane in the first place, now can you? However you look at it, they are both types of avoidance, and this stance is both unhealthy and unrealistic. I believe that we need to be changing this outlook of avoidance to one of preparedness.

None of us want to live day-in day-out in preparation for dealing with a terrorist attack, large-scale accident, or catastrophic event of any kind, but we can certainly do our bit to be ready should any of these things happen. It's my wish to develop Heads Up CIO to ensure that, whatever traumas may come our way, we can be ready to deal with them in the most positive way. After all, avoidance is the route of most, if not all, mental health disorders people go through.

They say that prevention is better than cure, and there is so much truth to this statement. Whilst we can never prevent what is out of our control and in the free will of others or some higher spiritual design, there is still a message to take from the 'prevention is better than cure' sentiment when it comes to our health. Mental health should be treated in the exact same way and taken just as seriously as physical health, and I hope that this book goes on to raise that awareness.

We all know that preventative healthcare is more proactive than a response-based reaction, and that this approach yields longer-term benefits. For example, it's easier to keep an eye on your food intake and to exercise regularly all through your life, than to combat or recover from the associated negative health consequences that may follow because of a sedentary and poor dietary lifestyle, such as high cholesterol, heart disease or obesity. A sensible and preventative approach is more achievable for people, and certainly more sustainable, even though we fall foul again of that 'it won't happen to me' mentality in our approach.

In being prepared for anything in life, we are setting things in stone for our journeys (literal and figurative), our days and our ways of life. If we wait for something to happen before dealing with it, not only may we struggle with coping, adapting and recovering, but we may also, after a period, revert back to our old ways of either blissful or purposeful ignorance. This statement isn't intended to be judgemental, as such a slip is completely normal, but does that mean we should just carry on with that process?

The training that Heads Up CIO aims to offer as widely as we can in preparing people mentally for approaching and dealing with the effects of trauma and psychological shock in both themselves and others, is something that we want to embed into people's everyday practices so that it becomes automatic for them. I refer once again here to the scenario of flying. Have you ever flown on a plane? You may only do it once or twice a year, but you know the safety 'drill', so to speak. Do you always watch the safety demonstration? Even if you're not watching it because you're excitedly chattering about your trip with a companion, or you're busy sifting through your hand luggage for your headphones, or you're scoffing at the much-parodied 'here, here and here' demonstration, the information from this theatre always sinks in. It's repetitive and standardised, and that's exactly what it needs to be to become embedded in your thought process. It doesn't need to be creative, enigmatic or remotely inspiring, because it doesn't need to change your life; it needs to save it. Even if you haven't flown for years and you've never really taken note of what to do in an emergency since that first ever plane you set foot on, trust me, your brain hasn't switched off from that safety demonstration. It's taking it all in, and I'd put money on the fact that you know where your lifejacket is safely stored, you know how to tie it, and you know what to do if it doesn't inflate.

Should anything like last spring happen to us here in the UK again, I want to be a part of a movement that absolutely ensures that people know what to do in response, and so I need to make what Heads Up CIO can offer a part of everyday process and accessibility in people's lives.

Today could be 'the day before'. If those three weeks in 2017 are anything to go by or learn from, anything could happen at any time, and that of course doesn't even take into consideration more 'everyday' things that could occur and cause us to suffer trauma, such as accidents, natural disasters or violent crime. As a nation, the UK may not be at war, but we are involved in terrorism, in violence and in retaliation. Learning something like first aid (whether in the traditional form or the psychological aspect as detailed in this book), adds to a person's resilience on the day, should they ever need it. The more you learn and prepare, the more good you can and will do in handling yourself and supporting others in the confusing, upsetting and unsettling aftermath of traumatic events. There's an efficacy of knowing what to do. It's a much-needed confidence, and it's my hope and dream that this becomes a way of life, as opposed to something you struggle and panic to recall in a given time.

It's my belief that, in any situation regarding life, death and wellbeing, if you can do something to help, then no matter how small it might seem, you should do it. The earlier an action is applied, the better, and so the earlier we can teach these most positive of protocols regarding cognitive psychological first aid, the better.

A lot of people might view the training on offer as a form of stress management, and although there's a lot of truth to that, I feel that it's unfair to always use the word 'stress' in such negative terms. I believe that just as fear can be a good thing in protecting us from harm, stress can also be a good thing in terms of the fact that it can challenge us and push us onwards. Climbing Mount Everest, for example, must be a stressful trek to plan and navigate, but think of the achievement at the end! Not everybody would take on such a challenge owing to the physical and mental stresses it would present, but as with anything, if it was easy, then everybody would be doing it, and the excitement and novelty would be redundant. Challenge gone. If approached in a strategic way and managed properly, stress can be a good thing, and that's why I want to zone in on the stresses people are subjected to in a potentially traumatic situation and give them the skills and techniques they need to manage their own state as well as the state and wellbeing of others. It's all about getting to a place of cognition, where you can think clearly and act appropriately to keep yourself physically as well as mentally safe and functioning.

As you may remember from the start of this book, for part of my studies during my degree in social work I worked on the wards of a psychiatric hospital where I would come face to face daily with dual diagnosis patients, meaning they had both acute psychosis and substance use disorders. These were secure wards, and they were home to some of the least functioning human beings that you could think of. To end the description here, however, would be unfair, because everyone was still a human being, and each individual still had a value. In getting to know these people, I was taught some serious lessons about relationships and love, but perhaps that's the material for a whole new book entirely. Trust me, though, it would open your eyes. To say the least, the whole experience made me very aware of the fact that we all have dark and non-functioning moments, even if these do not form the DNA of our everyday lives. We all have these phases, and in dealing with a victim of shock through what we do at Heads Up CIO, I have learned how important it is to treat that person as a human being, rather than as a patient. It's a process, rather than a therapy. It should be 'everyday', not specialist. Even the word 'victim' could be contentious. In doing what we do, everybody is human, and it's important to get people into a state where they can function as one. It's a sense of empowerment, a sense of control, and a sense of being able to, well, carry on.

How will I carry on now that this book has been released and the work of Heads Up CIO is gaining in recognition and reputation? My aim is to utilise the publication as an essential tool in spreading our Heads Up CIO messages, and as a platform from which I can showcase the work that we do and the importance of its effects. I have always enjoyed attending events to hear my heroes speak, and so it is a wonderful point to consider that I may hopefully be able to inspire someone else in turn as I take on the mantle of being on the other side of that delivery podium!

So, where does this leave us right now as an organisation? As you read in a previous chapter, after two failed attempts at applying for formal funding from recognised funding organisations, Heads Up CIO made a third application. This time, it was to the National Lottery 'Awards for All' grant scheme. The name needs little more explanation than that, but obviously, with the parameters being quite generic in terms of who could apply and what could be funded, the competition was incredibly high. Having taken some lessons from the previous two applications, we were confident that Awards for All could be the grant that we could secure to put forward a programme of training and events that would help Heads Up CIO in our mission to prepare individuals and communities in resilience and response. The money we sought from Awards for All would be earmarked for 'HERE', which is a powerful acronym for a programme representing Health, Empowerment, Resilience and Engagement. The programme is aimed primarily at community bases and educational establishments at all levels. Schools may be the future, but university students are the demographic group better placed to make a speedier change, and so gaining access to both to deliver our training will be so important as we go about our work.

Prior to submitting this book to the publisher, I was excited to receive a letter from National Lottery HQ, in light of the Awards for All grant. I am delighted to tell our readers that the letter informed me we had been awarded the maximum grant amount of £10,000 for Heads Up CIO. As you turn each page of this book, those funds are being put to immediate and effective use in training up the next cohorts of people who, one day, may save your life. Jonny Wineberg is my friend and colleague to whom I am forever grateful in doing everything in his power to make sure we received this wonderful news.

So, as we end, what was the purpose of this book? Well, it was never intended to be a manual, and it certainly didn't start out life as any kind of autobiographical work. If the pages contained within it provide process and reassurance as a result, however, then this is no bad thing.

I wanted the stories that weaved in and out of the events that were taking place in the UK in the spring of

2017 – the Spring of Unease as I now refer to it – to be informative and engaging to the point where it would inspire people to act and to get involved. Whilst it may well be of entertainment value (and let's face it, nobody wants to be bored by a book), the ideal emotive response is for people to get up, get out and get going in terms of developing their resilience and empowering others using techniques in and around the concept of CORTEX-CPFA.

Although I stand by the fact that I am in no way an academic, there's no getting away from the fact that I am a big reader. I enjoy non-fiction books, mostly, and take great enjoyment from publications that I can pick up and put down at any point without losing an opportunity to take away an element of learning or insight. That's what I wanted this book to serve as when I first sat down to plan it. Sure, there will be elements that are purely documentary, but I would hope that even in those narrative passages, readers will be able to take away some learning about leadership, operation, or perhaps even the human condition. I hope that this book will inspire action and evoke nurturing change, either for individuals or for larger communities. Hopefully, both.

I have always been inspired by my mentors in the worlds of therapy and teaching, and so I am hoping that I can inspire others in the same fashion with this book. I do not hope to be 'the big name' in association with CORTEX-CPFA, but I do hope that Heads Up CIO is the go-to organisation for paving the way in good practice and pioneering the most progressive techniques in the support and treatment of those affected by stress, trauma and psychological shock.

I don't expect every reader to finish this book and get straight online to check out the details for Heads Up CIO, but if people want to do that, I'm not going to turn down anyone who can help us logistically or who wants to get involved in our training. In contrast, I am more hopeful that this book will be the first step a person can take to truly prepare themselves mentally, and to take better care of themselves and others as a result of them witnessing or being involved in an event that affects them so profoundly in terms of their mental state and wellbeing.

Whilst I wish for the future to bring as much positivity as possible through the work of Heads Up CIO, 2017 was a year that tested me in every way imaginable. I went without sleep and I went without a clue into unfamiliar territories. I witnessed the cruellest events and encountered the kindest hearts. I learned about building a charity and I learned about developing myself.

The book is something I absolutely needed to invest my time, energy and resource into, but honestly, I wish we lived in a world where I never had to write this book in the first place.

RECOGNITION AND THANK YOU!

One Love Manchester was a benefit concert and British television special held on 4 June 2017, which was organised by American singer and actress Ariana Grande in response to the bombing after her concert at Manchester Arena two weeks earlier. The concert was attended by 55,000 people [https://en.wikipedia.org/wiki/One_Love_Manchester].

On this day, Heads Up CIO dispatched it's UK national emergency response, resilience and support service for stress and trauma to the concert with two main aims:

1. To give support to those nervously attending this concert only two weeks after the bombing of her concert at Manchester Arena.
2. To be on-hand and available in the event of an emergency incident.

This was the first time in the UK that such a proactive and preventative psycho-trauma team had ever been activated at a public event.

Recognition and special thanks should be given to this historical event and special team members led by Dov Benyaacov-Kurtzman, for their bravery, willingness, compassion and hard work.

Jo Almond
Olivia Baker
Vicky Bowen
Anne Cartridge
Siobhan Cooper
Ryan Crooks
Penelope Deane
Mel Denniss
Jordan Driver
Jacqueline Korn
Geoff Kwartz
Haley Leigh
Tricia Malone
Damian Mayoh
Briony Seed
Steven Yale

To contact Dov Benyaacov-Kurtzman for more information regarding getting involved with Heads Up CIO, training, interviews, public speaking events or to volunteer, you may contact him at the following email address:

hello@headsupcio.org.uk
UKNationalResilience.com
headsupcio.org.uk

The first few minutes and hours of psycho-trauma care are critical to achieving better outcomes. *FACT – UK National Psycho-trauma Practical Training School* is dedicated to bringing to the UK state-of-the-art psycho-trauma care training, empowering professionals and laypersons with the knowledge, critical thinking skills, and hands-on training to provide expert care for those affected by psycho-trauma due to terrorist attacks and other major disasters – natural and man-made. We want to ensure that the people of the United Kingdom are prepared. By developing resilience within our communities, together we can become stronger and reduce anxiety.

+44 (0) 161 241 2382
factcpfa@gmail.com

Emergency vest

Dov and Louise Hayes

*Dov and Peter Aldous MP in
Westminster*

Prosocial Act training for Heads Up CIO volunteers

Front cover of Mishpacha Magazine

Heads Up CIO sign